BONEY M.

All The Top 40 Hits

Craig Halstead

Copyright © Craig Halstead 2019

All rights reserved. No part of this publication may be reproduced, stored in a retrieval system, or transmitted in any form or by any means, electronic, mechanical, photocopy, recording or otherwise, without prior written permission of the copyright owner. Nor can it be circulated in any form of binding or cover other than that in which it is published and without similar condition including this condition being imposed on a subsequent purchaser.

First Edition

By the same author

Christmas Number Ones

The 'All The Top 40 Hits' Series

ABBA
Carpenters
Janet Jackson
Michael Jackson
Olivia Newton-John

The 'For The Record' Series

Donna Summer
Janet Jackson
Michael Jackson
Whitney Houston

Fiction

Tyranny
The Secret Library (James Harris 1)
Shadow Of Death (James Harris 2)
Cataclysm Book 1: The First 73 Days
Cataclysm Book 2: A New Year

www.craighalstead.com

for Aaron

ACKNOWLEDGEMENTS

I would like to thank Chris Cadman, my writing partner, for helping to make my writing dreams come true. It's incredible to think how far we have come, since we got together to compile 'The Complete Michael Jackson Discography 1972-1990', for Adrian Grant's *Off the Wall* fan magazine in 1990. Now, of course, we're both working on solo projects ~ I'm already looking forward to reading your next one!

I would also like to thank the online music community, who so readily share and exchange information at: ukmix (ukmix.org/forums), Haven (fatherandy2.proboards.com) & Buzzjack (buzzjack.com/forums). In particular, I would like to thank:

- 'BrainDamagell' & 'Wayne' for posting current USA & Canadian charts on ukmix;
- 'flatdeejay' & 'ChartFreaky' for posting German chart action, and 'Indi' for answering my queries regarding Germany, on ukmix;
- 'Davidalic' for posting Spanish chart action on ukmix;
- 'Shakyfan', 'CZB' & 'beatlened' for posting Irish charts on ukmix;
- 'Hanboo' for posting and up-dating on request full UK & USA chart runs on ukmix. R.I.P., Hanboo ~ like everyone on ukmix, I was shocked and deeply saddened to learn of your passing.
- 'trebor' for posting pre-1983 Swiss singles and albums charts on ukmix.
- 'janjensen' for posting Danish singles charts from 1979 onwards on ukmix.

If you can fill any of the gaps in the chart information in this book, or have chart runs from a country not already featured in the book, I would love to hear from you. You can contact me via **www.craighalstead.com** ~ thank you!

CONTENTS

INTRODUCTION	7
ALL THE TOP 40 SINGLES	25
THE ALMOST TOP 40 SINGLES	119
TOP 20 BONEY M. SINGLES	120
SINGLES TRIVIA	123
ALL THE TOP 40 ALBUMS	137
TOP 20 BONEY M. ALBUMS	203
ALBUMS TRIVIA	205

INTRODUCTION

In most countries, Boney M. burst on to the music scene in 1976 with *Daddy Cool* ~ not the first single credited to the group, but the first actually attributed to the four recognised members of the group.

Boney M. was the creation of Frank Farian, a German singer/producer, and the group went through several line-up changes before the three women/one man quartet that found international fame came together. Frank, although he wasn't officially part of the group, was integral to the success of Boney M.

'I have always said it was a big accident,' Frank observed. 'Liz says it's God. It all come together perfectly in four weeks.'

The four members of Boney M. who made promotional appearances and appeared in concert together were:

- Liz Mitchell
- Marcia Barrett
- Maizie Williams
- Bobby Farrell

In the studio and on record, however, Boney M. was actually a trio:

- Frank Farian
- Liz Mitchell
- Marcia Barrett

Maizie and Bobby were initially recruited as dancers, and they made no vocal contribution to Boney M.'s studio recordings, with producer Frank responsible for all the group's distinctive male vocals.

Frank Farian

Franz Reuther was born in Kim, Germany, on 18th July 1951. He started out as a *schlager* singer, *schlager* being a German style of pop music with happy-go-lucky, often sentimental vocals, with catchy instrumentation.

As Frankie Farian, Franz released his debut single – a cover of Otis Redding's *Mr. Pitiful* – in 1967, and over the next decade he released numerous singles, most of them in continental Europe only. His biggest success came in April 1976, when his single *Rocky* hit no.1 in Germany ~ just five months before Boney M. did the same with *Daddy Cool*.

Before he found success with *Rocky*, Frank Farian as he was now known wrote and recorded the disco song *Baby, Do You Wanna Bump* under the pseudonym Boney M., as it was so different from his own material. The non-existent group was named after an Australia detective show, *Boney*.

'I turned on the TV one day and it was the end of a detective series,' said Frank. 'I just caught the credits and it said 'Boney'. Nice name, I thought – Boney, Boney, Boney ... Boney M. Boney, Boney, Boney M. Nice sound. Simple.'

When *Baby, Do You Wanna Bump* entered the charts in Belgium and the Netherlands, Frank faced a dilemma: he didn't want to promote the single himself, as it didn't fit in with his image as a *schlager* singer, but Boney M. didn't actually exist. He quickly decided to form a group, to front discotheque and TV performances, and invited three young woman and one young man to appear as Boney M., to dance and lip-synch to *Baby, Do You Wanna Bump*.

'For fifteen years I'd sung and sung and never had a hit,' Frank commented. 'Of course, I realise that my importance in the group could be devalued, but I can't be bothered because we are selling records.'

The four original members of Boney M. were Maizie Williams, her friend Sheyla, plus Nathalie and Mike.

Three of the original line-up soon departed, and eventually a new, settled line-up was confirmed: Maizie Williams, Marcia Barrett, Bobby Farrell and Liz Mitchell. However, of the four, only two made a vocal contribution to Boney M.'s debut album and subsequent releases: Marcia and Liz. In Frank's opinion, Maizie's and Bobby's vocals weren't suited to Boney M.'s style of music, and he provided all the male vocals heard on record himself. However, both Maizie and Bobby did sing with Boney M., when they performed their numerous live concerts.

During the second half of the 1970s, Boney M. was immensely successful all around the world, but as the 1980s dawned, so the hits – especially the very big hits – started to wane.

In 1981, a result of his unreliability, Frank fired Bobby, which meant the group were unable to properly promote their fifth studio album, *BOONOONOONOOS*. Bobby was replaced by singer Reggie Tsiboe but, as their success faded, so Frank began to lose interest in Boney M., and his focus switched to other projects – most notably and most notoriously, Milli Vanilli, a duo whose success suddenly nose-dived when it was revealed they weren't actually singing on their records.

Over the years, Frank has released numerous edits and remixes of Boney M. recordings, on numerous compilation albums, most of which haven't sold well enough to chart anywhere.

Maizie Williams

Maizie Ursula Williams was born in Brades, Montserrat, an island in the Caribbean, on 25th March 1951. She was raised in Birmingham, England, and even as a young girl she always wanted to be involved in show business in some way. She started out as a model, having been to modelling classes, and she won the title Miss Black Beautiful in 1973. The same year, she fronted her own band, Black Beautiful People.

Maizie took dancing classes, and started dancing and acting, as well as modelling. She was in Germany with her friend Sheyla Bonnick, for a fashion show, when they were approached by Frank Farian's agent, and asked if they were interested in joining a new pop group.

'It was strange,' said Maizie. 'Two days before we were supposed to take off and come back to England, I was approached about joining a group called Boney M.. For me it was the most incredible thing that ever happened. I've always believed in destiny, I'm quite superstitious, but this was something different.'

Maizie and Sheyla were joined by a young woman called Nathalie and a young man called Mike. Together, the foursome were pictured on early promotional photographs of Boney M., toured discotheques and appeared on TV, dancing and miming to Frank Farian's Boney M. hit, *Baby, Do You Wanna Bump*.

Nathalie soon left the group, and was replaced by Claudja Barry. Sheyla and Mike were the next to leave, and their places in the fledgling group were taken by singer Marcia Barrett and dancer Bobby Farrell. Then Claudja left as well, and her replacement – singer Liz Mitchell – was the final piece in the jigsaw, and the group that found international success as Boney M. was born.

Frank Farian didn't feel Maizie's voice was suited to Boney M., so all the female vocals were recorded by Marcia and Liz, with the latter's distinctive vocals soon recognised the world over as the sound of Boney M.. Maizie did, however, sing during Boney M.'s many live concerts around the world, as did Bobby.

Four years after Boney M. split for good in 1990, as Liz and Bobby had already done, Maizie formed her own version of Boney M., billed as Boney M. featuring Maizie Williams.

Maizie took Frank Farian and Sony/BMG to court, to assert her right to perform under the name 'Boney M., and in February 2009 the judgement went in her favour. Further, Frank Farian was instructed to pay Maizie for all Boney M. record sales and future sales.

Boney M.

BROWN GIRL IN THE RING | DADDY COOL | RASPUTIN | SUNNY
MA BAKER | HOORAY HOORAY ITS A HOLIDAY | PAINTER MAN
GOTTA GO HOME | RIVERS OF BABYLON

40 YEARS OF DISCO - CHRISTMAS SPECIAL

CARDIFF | ST DAVIDS HALL
SAT 01 DEC 2018

Box office: 029 2087 8444 | www.stdavidshallcardiff.co.uk

Maizie released her debut solo album, *CALL UPON JESUS*, in 2006. The following year, she was the featured vocalist on Latvian cello trio Melo M's cover of *Daddy Cool*, which went to no.1 in Latvia, and her version of Boney M. continues to tour to this day.

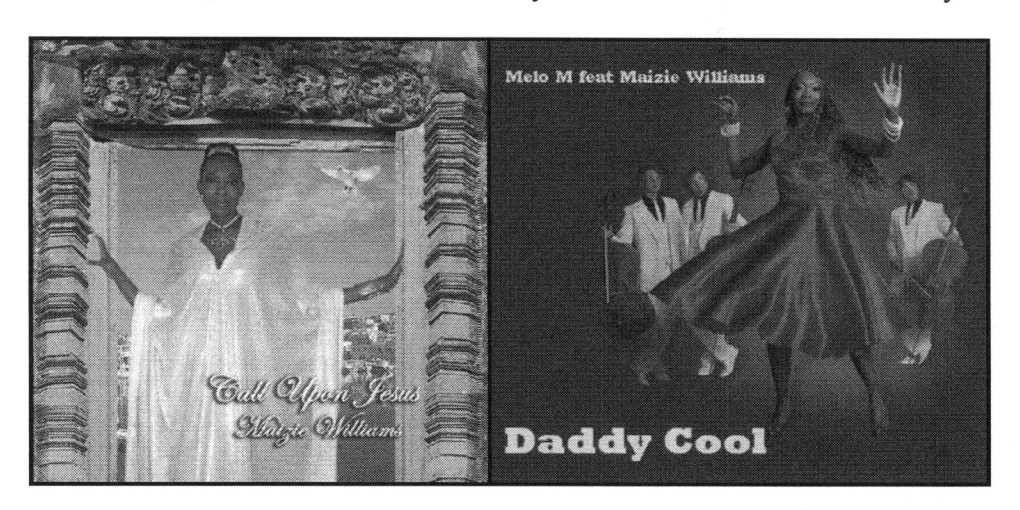

Marcia Barrett

Marcia Barrett was born in St. Catherine, Jamaica, on 14th October 1948.

She and her family came to Croydon, England, in 1963, and in the late 1960s she moved to Germany, where she formed a band and toured with Karel Gott and Rex Gildo. She signed to Metronome Records in 1971, and her debut single *Could Be Love* was released later the same year, but it wasn't a hit.

Marcia joined Boney M. in 1975 and, when Claudja Barry left the group, it was Marcia who recommended Liz Mitchell as her replacement.

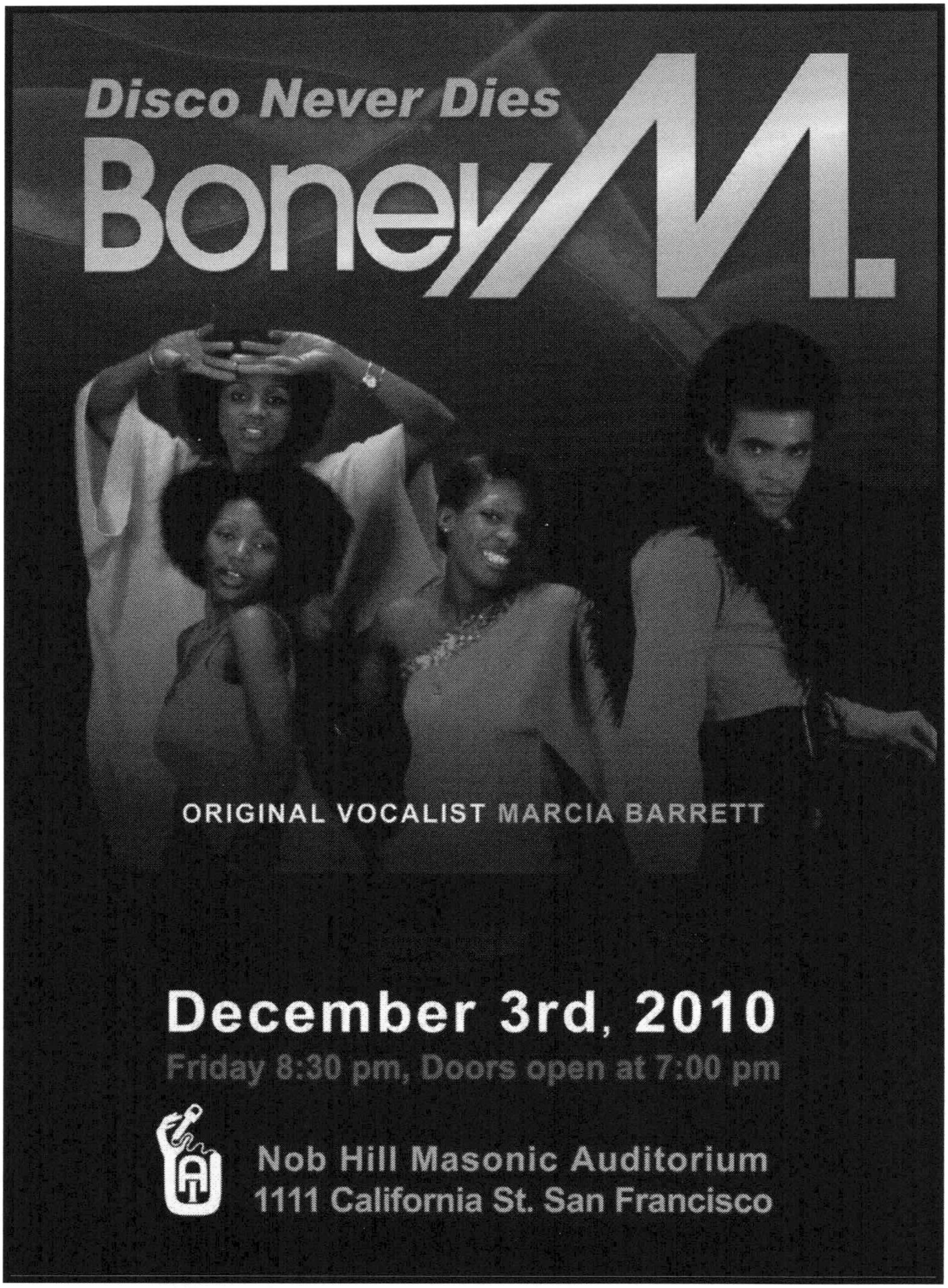

Disco Never Dies
Boney M.
ORIGINAL VOCALIST MARCIA BARRETT
December 3rd, 2010
Friday 8:30 pm, Doors open at 7:00 pm
Nob Hill Masonic Auditorium
1111 California St. San Francisco

Boney M's most successful albums were recorded by Marcia, Liz and Frank Farian, and on the group's debut album, *TAKE THE HEAT OFF ME*, Marcia sang lead vocals on the title track and *Lovin' Or Leavin'*. These two songs, credited to Marcia Barrett, were released as a single in 1977 in a small number of countries, including Germany, Greece and Italy, but failed to chart anywhere.

Although most people recognise Liz Mitchell as Boney M.'s lead singer, Marcia did contribute lead vocals on several tracks, including the hit singles *Belfast* and *We Kill The World (Don't Kill The World)*. She also shared lead vocals with Liz on a number of hits, including *Ma Baker*, *Rasputin* and *Gotta Go Home*.

In the late 1980s, Marcia attempted to launch a solo career, while remaining a member of Boney M.. She released one single, titled *You*, with Frank Farian's blessing, but she blamed its lack of success on Frank's failure to promote the single.

Vocally, Marcia made very little contribution to Boney M.'s final two studio albums, *TEN THOUSAND LIGHTYEARS* and *EYE DANCE*. Liz Mitchell left Boney M. during the group's 1989 tour, and was replaced by Madeleine Davis. However, when Frank made it known he had no plans to record new music with Boney M., the new line-up went to France, and recorded *Everybody Wants To Dance Like Josephine Baker* with producer Barry Blue. A hit seemed likely, until Frank forced the single's withdrawal, angry the group had recorded as Boney M. without him, thus breaking the terms of their contract.

After a court case in 1990, Marcia and the other members of Boney M. went their separate ways. Marcia was keen to resurrect her solo career, but it was tough going: she was diagnosed with cancer not once, not twice, but five times. And five times she battled the awful disease, and won. In her words: 'Life after Boney M. – my dear, I've been through hell and back.'

Fighting cancer meant, of course, Marcia spent nowhere near as much time recording, singing and touring as she would have liked, but over the years she has released two solo albums, the appropriately titled *SURVIVAL* in 1999, and *COME INTO MY LIFE* in 2005.

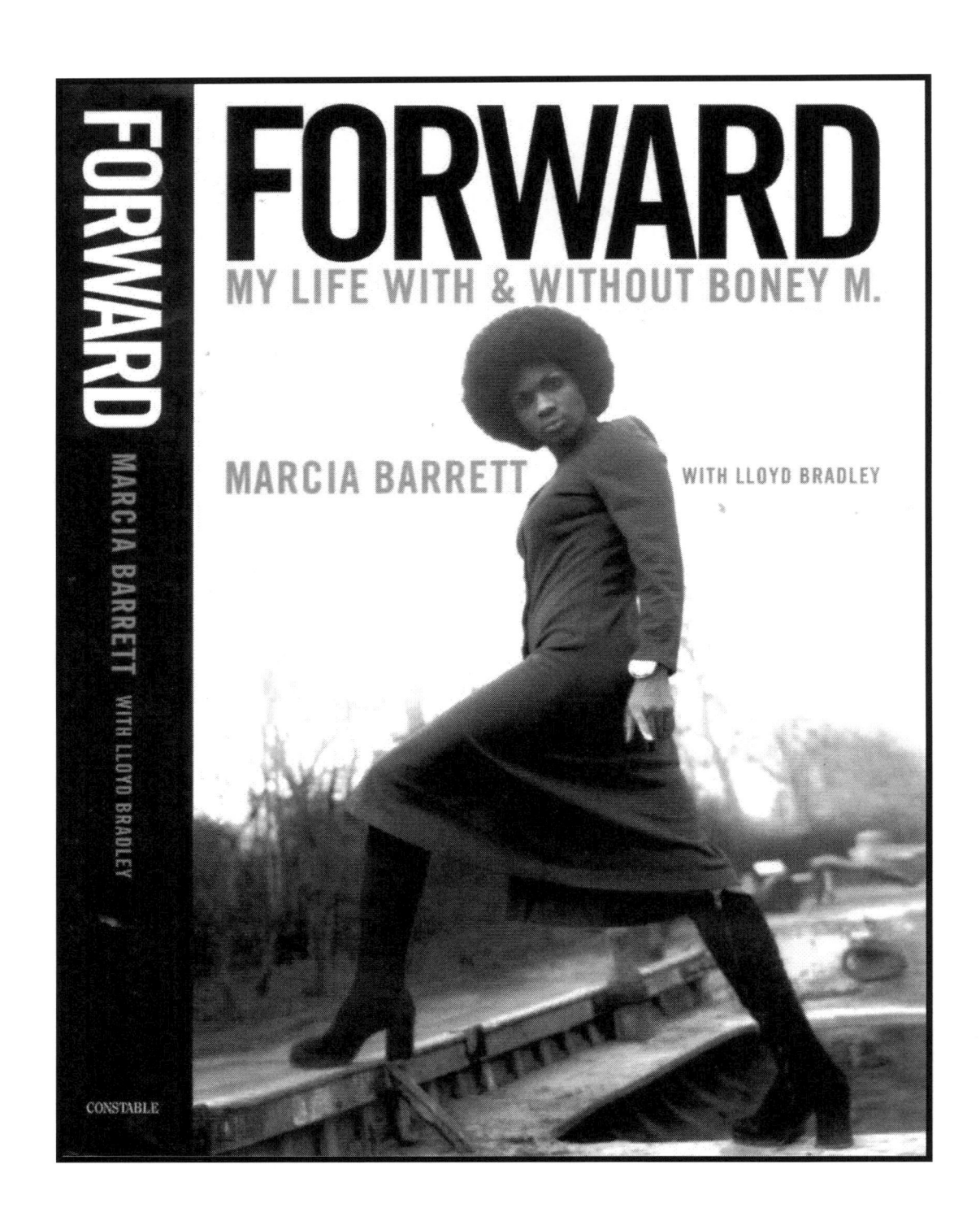

FORWARD
MY LIFE WITH & WITHOUT BONEY M.

MARCIA BARRETT WITH LLOYD BRADLEY

CONSTABLE

Marcia's autobiography, *FORWARD – My Life With & Without Boney M.*, was published in 2018, in both English and German editions.

Bobby Farrell

Roberto Alfonso 'Bobby' Farrell was born in San Nicolaas, Aruba, on 6th October 1949. After leaving school, he spent two years working as a sailor, before he moved to Norway, then the Netherlands, and finally Germany, where he found opportunities to work as a dancer and a DJ.

Bobby, like Maizie Williams, was recruited to Boney M. principally as a dancer and, like her, he made no vocal contribution at all to the group's recordings. The male voice heard on most of Boney M.'s hits and albums belonged to group's producer, Frank Farian. However, like Maizie, Bobby did contribute vocally to Boney M.'s live concerts.

'Even before we had a hit,' said Bobby, 'we had four nights work a week, so I was happy enough. He (Frank Farian) took us to his home and played us the tracks to *Daddy Cool*, *Sunny*, *No Woman, No Cry* and stuff like that.'

Away from Boney M., Bobby recorded a duet with the Austrian singer Gilla in 1977, which was co-written and produced by Frank Farian. Titled *Gentlemen Callers Not Allowed*, it was only released in the Netherlands, where it was a Top 20 hit. Five years on, Bobby released a solo single, *Polizei*, but it wasn't a hit. Another five years, and he had a minor hit in the Netherlands with *Hoppa Hoppa*.

Citing his unreliability, Frank fired Bobby from Boney M. in 1981, and replaced him with singer Reggie Tsiboe. Bobby rejoined the group in 1984, and stayed until Boney M. split in 1986.

Bobby formed his own group, which he called Bobby Farrell's Boney M., and continued to tour and perform Boney M. hits. He also released several compilation albums, featuring new recordings of songs Boney M. had made famous.

Bobby complained of breathing problems, after performing a concert in Saint Petersburg, Russia, on 29th December 2010. The following morning, when he failed to respond to an alarm call, he was found dead in his hotel room. The cause of death was given as heart failure.

Bobby was buried at Zorgvlied Cemetery in Amsterdam, Netherlands, where he had made his home. Maizie Williams, Marcia Barrett and Liz Mitchell all attended his funeral.

Liz Mitchell

Elizabeth Rebecca 'Liz' Mitchell was born in Clarendon, Jamaica, on 12th July 1952. Her family moved to London, England, in 1963 when Liz was 11.

Towards the end of the 1960s, Liz auditioned for the German production of the musical *Hair*, and was successful. She moved to Berlin, where she replaced Donna Summer in the musical, before spending several years with the Les Humphries Singers. Liz, who had met her while in Germany, was brought to Frank Farian's attention by Marcia Barrett, and she became the final piece in the Boney M. jigsaw.

Liz sang lead vocals on the majority of Boney M.'s recordings, including many of their biggest hits, and is generally recognised as the distinctive voice behind Boney M.. As Frank Farian once observed, 'All members could be replaced, except Liz.'

Boney M. celebrated their 10th anniversary in 1986, by which time the hits had more or less dried up, and shortly afterwards the group split. Frank Farian persuaded Liz and Maizie Williams to get together again, and tour in 1987 with a replacement for Marcia Barrett. A new record contract was agreed, however, both Frank and Marcia's replacement failed to show to record planned new songs so, as Maizie had never actually sung on any Boney M. recordings, Liz went ahead and recorded what became her debut solo album, *NO ONE WILL FORCE YOU*, which was originally released in Spain towards the end of 1988. Two singles, *Mandela* (a re-working of the Boney M. hit, *El Lute*) and *Niños De La Playa* (Children On The Beach), were released but both failed to chart.

RECORD MIRROR

June 10, 1978

Kiss, Springsteen albums Genesis XTC

BONEY M IN ROME

TOTP v Revolver
Mickie Most & Robin Nash clash

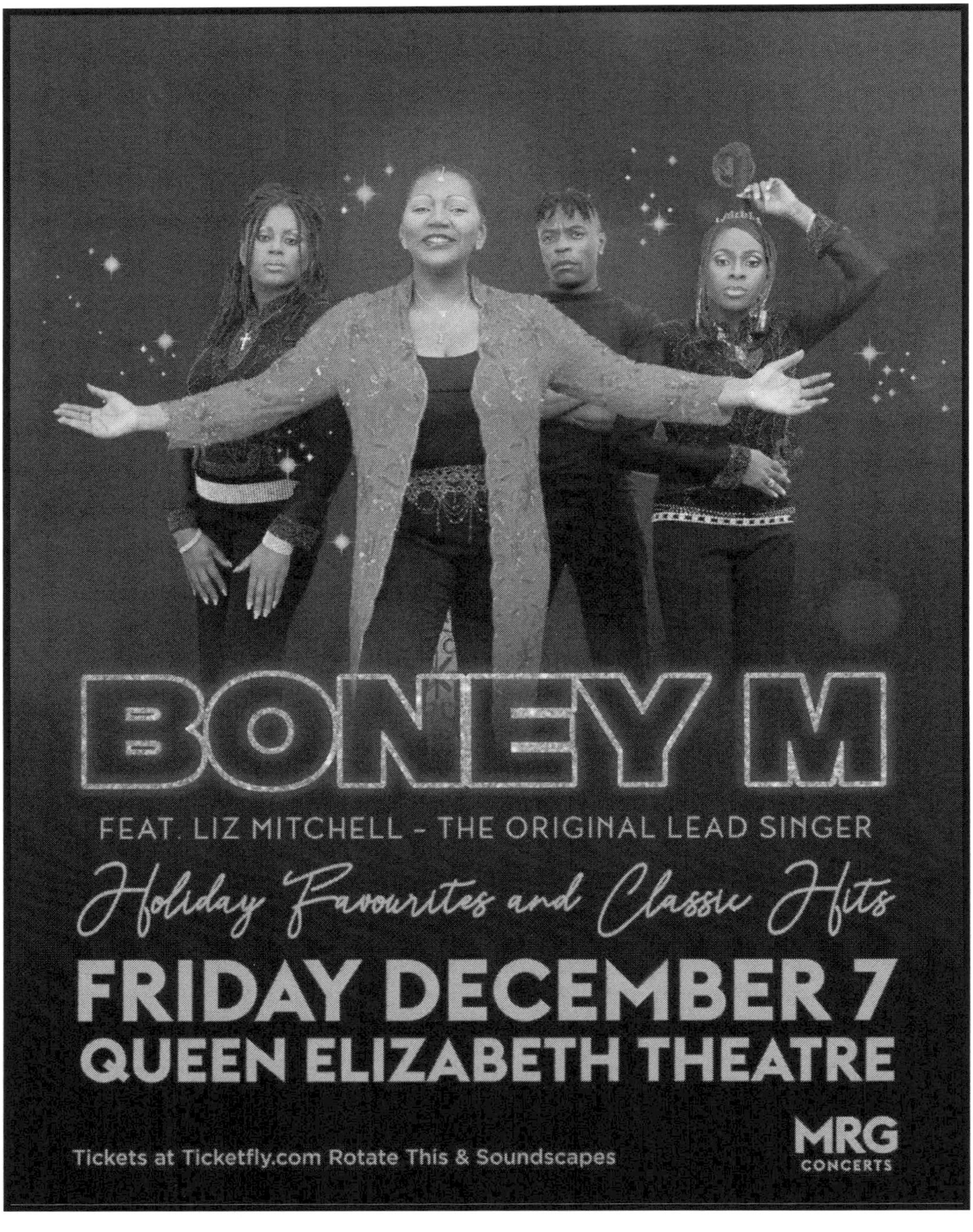
BONEY M
FEAT. LIZ MITCHELL - THE ORIGINAL LEAD SINGER
Holiday Favourites and Classic Hits
FRIDAY DECEMBER 7
QUEEN ELIZABETH THEATRE
Tickets at Ticketfly.com Rotate This & Soundscapes
MRG CONCERTS

Somewhat reluctantly, Liz agreed to re-join Marcia Barrett, Maizie Williams and Bobby Farrell, to promote the remix album, *GREATEST HITS OF ALL TIMES – REMIX '88*, which returned Boney M. to the chart in many countries. The album's success meant a Volume II duly followed, but it sold poorly by comparison, and what proved to be Boney M.'s final new single, *Stories* – Frank Farian's answer to *Everybody Wants To Dance Like Josephine Baker* – was only a minor hit.

In 1996, Liz and her husband Thomas Pemberton formed their own record label, Dove House Records, and as a thank you to her fans Liz re-recorded four of Boney M. Christmas songs, and released them as a maxi-CD single. The four songs were: *When A Child Is Born*, *Zion's Daughter*, *Feliz Navidad* and *Mary's Boy Child / Oh My Lord*.

Since 1996, Liz has released four solo albums, and more recently one credited to Boney M. feat. Liz Mitchell and Friends:

- *SHARE THE WORLD* (1999).
- *A CHRISTMAS ROSE* (2000).
- *LET IT BE* (2004).
- *SINGS THE HITS OF BONEY M.* (2005).
- *WORLD MUSIC FOR CHRISTMAS* (2017).

Liz continues to tour to this day, billed as Boney M. featuring Liz Mitchell.

Reggie Tsiboe

Reggie Tsiboe was born in Kumasi, Ghana, on 7th September 1950.

Before coming to the UK, Reggie was a movie star in his native Ghana. Before joining Boney M. in 1982, to replace Bobby Farrell, he released two solo singles, *Please Don't Tell Your Sister* in 1974, and *Wendy* three years later ~ neither was a hit.

When Bobby re-joined Boney M. in 1984, Reggie stayed on as well, and the group expanded to a quintet. The following year, with the Frank Farian Corporation, he released a cover of Paul Simon's *Mother And Child Reunion*, but it wasn't a hit.

The new Boney M. line-up only lasted two years and, after their 10th anniversary concert, the members of the group decided to go their separate ways.

Reggie formed a new, official version of Boney M. with Liz Mitchell in 1989, but the new group lasted less than a year, and after it disbanded Reggie returned to acting.

All The Top 40 Hits

For the purposes of this book, to qualify as a Top 40 hit, a single or album must have entered the Top 40 singles/albums chart in at least one of eighteen featured countries: Australia, Austria, Belgium, Canada, Denmark, Finland, France, Germany, Ireland (singles only), Japan, the Netherlands, New Zealand, Norway, Spain, Sweden, Switzerland, the United Kingdom and the United States of America.

The Top 40 singles and albums are detailed chronologically, according to the date they first entered the chart in one or more of the featured countries. Each Top 40 single and album is illustrated and the catalogue numbers and release dates are detailed, for both the Germany and the UK, followed by the chart runs in each featured country, including any chart re-entries. Where full chart runs are unavailable, peak position and weeks on the chart are given.

For singles, the main listing is followed by 'The Almost Top 40 Singles', which gives an honourable mention to Boney M. singles that peaked between no.41 and no.50 in one or more countries (no Boney M. albums did the same). There is also a points-based list of the Top 20 Boney M. Singles and Albums, plus a fascinating 'Trivia' section at the end of each section which looks at the most successful Boney M. singles and albums in each of the featured countries.

The Charts

The charts from an increasing number of countries are now freely available online, and for many countries it is possible to research weekly chart runs. Although this book focuses on Top 40 hits, longer charts runs are included where available, up to the Top 100 for countries where a Top 100 or longer is published.

Nowadays, charts are compiled and published on a weekly basis – in the past, however, some countries published charts on a bi-weekly or monthly basis, and most charts listed far fewer titles than they do today. There follows a summary of the current charts from each country featured in this book, together with relevant online resources and chart books.

Australia
Current charts: Top 100 Singles & Top 100 Albums.
Online resources: current weekly Top 50 Singles & Albums, but no archive, at **ariacharts.com.au**; archive of complete weekly charts dating back to 2001 at **pandora.nla.gov.au/tep/23790**; searchable archive of Top 50 Singles & Albums dating back to 1988 at **australian-charts.com**.
Books: 'Australian Chart Book 1970-1992' & 'Australian Chart Book 1993-2009' by David Kent.

Austria
Current charts: Top 75 Singles & Top 75 Albums.
Online resources: current weekly charts and a searchable archive dating back to 1965 for singles and 1973 for albums at **austriancharts.at**.

Belgium
Current charts: Top 50 Singles & Top 200 Albums for two different regions, Flanders (the Dutch speaking north of the country) and Wallonia (the French speaking south).
Online resources: current weekly charts and a searchable archive dating back to 1995 for albums, and pre-1976 for singles, at **ultratop.be**.
Book: '*Het Belgisch Hitboek – 40 Jaar Hits In Vlaanderen*' by Robert Collin.
Note: the information in this book for Belgium relates to the Flanders region.

Canada
Current charts: Hot 100 Singles & Top 100 Albums.
Online resources: weekly charts and a searchable archive of weekly charts from the Nielsen SoundScan era at **billboard.com/biz** (subscription only); incomplete archive of weekly RPM charts dating back to 1964 for singles and 1967 for albums at **collectionscanada.gc.ca/rpm** (RPM folded in 2000).
Book: 'The Canadian Singles Chart Book 1975-1996' by Nanda Lwin.

Denmark
Current Charts: Top 40 Singles & Albums.

Online resources: weekly charts and a fully searchable archive at **danishcharts.com**, however, this only goes back to 2001. In 2001, the chart was a weekly Top 20, which expanded to a Top 40 in November 2007. No archive currently exists for charts before 2001. 'CZB' has posted weekly Top 20s from September 1994 to December 1999 on **ukmix.org**, and 'janjensen' has posted the Top 10 singles from January 1979 onwards on the same forum. This means no album charts before September 1994 are available, and there is no information for 2000.

Finland
Current charts: Top 20 Singles & Top 50 Albums.
Online resources: current weekly charts and a searchable archive dating back to 1995 at **finnishcharts.com**.

France
Current charts: Top 200 Singles & Top 200 Albums.
Online resources: current weekly charts and a searchable archive dating back to 1984 for singles and 1997 for albums at **lescharts.com**; searchable, unofficial archive for earlier/other charts at **infodisc.fr**.
Book: '*Hit Parades 1950-1998*' by Daniel Lesueur.
Note: Compilation albums were excluded from the main chart until 2008, when a Top 200 Comprehensive chart was launched.

Germany
Current charts: Top 100 Singles & Top 100 Albums.
Online resources: current weekly charts (Top 10s only) and a searchable archive dating back to 2007 (again, Top 10s only) at **germancharts.com**; complete Top 100 charts are usually posted weekly in the German Charts Thread on **ukmix.org**.
Books: '*Deutsche Chart Singles 1956-1980*', '*Deutsche Chart Singles 1981-90*', '*Deutsche Chart Singles 1991-1995*' & '*Deutsche Chart LP's 1962-1986*' published by Taurus Press.

Ireland
Current charts: Top 100 Singles & Top 100 Albums.
Online resources: current weekly charts are available at **irma.ie**; there is a searchable archive for Top 30 singles (entry date, peak position and week on chart only) at **irishcharts.ie**. Weekly singles chart from 1967 to 1999 have been posted in the Irish Chart Thread on **ukmix.org**.
Note: the Irish album chart launched much later than the singles chart, and there is no online archive, so only chart information for singles is included in this book.

Japan
Current charts: Top 200 Singles & Top 300 Albums.

Online resources: current weekly charts (in Japanese) at **oricon.co.jp/rank**; selected information is available on the Japanese Chart/The Newest Charts and Japanese Chart/The Archives threads at **ukmix.org**.

Netherlands
Current charts: Top 100 Singles & Top 100 Albums.
Online resources: current weekly charts and a searchable archive dating back to 1956 for singles and 1969 for albums at **dutchcharts.nl**.

New Zealand
Current charts: Top 40 Singles & Top 40 Albums.
Online resources: current weekly charts and a searchable archive dating back to 1975 at **charts.org.nz**.
Book: 'The Complete New Zealand Music Charts 1966-2006' by Dean Scapolo.

Norway
Current charts: Top 20 Singles & Top 40 Albums.
Online resources: current weekly charts and a searchable archive dating back to 1958 for singles and 1967 for albums at **norwegiancharts.com**.

South Africa
Current charts: no official charts.
Online resources: none known.
Book: *South Africa Chart Book* by Christopher Kimberley.
Note: the singles chart was discontinued in early 1989, as singles were no longer being manufactured in significant numbers. The albums chart only commenced in December 1981, and was discontinued in 1995, following re-structuring of the South African Broadcasting Corporation.

Spain
Current charts: Top 50 Singles & Top 100 Albums.
Online resources: current weekly charts and a searchable archive dating back to 2005 at **spanishcharts.com**.
Book: *'Sólo éxitos 1959-2002 Año a Año'* by Fernando Salaverri.

Sweden
Current charts: Top 60 Singles & Top 100 Albums.
Online resources: current weekly charts and a searchable archive dating back to 1975 at **swedishcharts.com**.

Switzerland
Current charts: Top 75 Singles & Top 100 Albums.
Online resources: current weekly charts and a searchable archive dating back to 1968 for singles and 1983 for albums at **hitparade.ch**. Pre-1983 album charts have been posted in the Chat Analysis section of ukmix (**ukmix.org**).

UK
Current Charts: Top 100 Singles & Top 200 Albums.
Online resources: current weekly Top 100 charts and a searchable archive dating back to 1960 at **officialcharts.com**; weekly charts are posted on a number of music forums, including ukmix (**ukmix.org**), Haven (**fatherandy2.proboards.com**) and Buzzjack (**buzzjack.com**).
Note: weekly Top 200 album charts are only available via subscription from UK ChartsPlus (**ukchartsplus.co.uk**).

USA
Current charts: Hot 100 Singles & Billboard 200 Albums.
Online resources: current weekly charts are available at **billboard.com**, however, to access Billboard's searchable archive at **billboard.com/biz** you must be a subscriber; weekly charts are posted on a number of music forums, including ukmix (**ukmix.org**), Haven (**fatherandy2.proboards.com**) and Buzzjack (**buzzjack.com**).

Zimbabwe
Current charts: no official charts.
Online resources: none known.
Books: *Zimbabwe Singles Chart Book* & *Zimbabwe Albums Chart Book* by Christopher Kimberley.
Note: Zimbabwe was, of course, known as Rhodesia before 1980, but the country is referred to by its present name throughout this book. The information presented in this book was obtained through personal correspondence with Christopher Kimberley, and from his books.

Note: In the past, there was often one or more weeks over Christmas and New Year when no new album chart was published in some countries. In such cases, the previous week's chart has been used to complete a chart run. Similarly, where a bi-weekly or monthly chart was in place, for chart runs these are counted at two and four weeks, respectively.

All The Top 40 Singles

1 ~ BABY, DO YOU WANNA BUMP

Germany: Hansa 13 834 AT (1975).
  B-side: *Baby, Do You Wanna Bump (Part II)*.

UK: Creole CR 119 (1976).
  B-side: *Baby, Do You Wanna Bump (Part II)*.

Baby, Do You Wanna Bump wasn't a hit in Germany or the UK.

Belgium (Flanders)
17.01.76: 22-12-**8-8**-10-19-26

Netherlands
3.01.76: 23-**12-12**-16

Based on Prince Buster's 1964 recording, *Al Capone*, Frank Farian wrote *Baby, Do You Wanna Bump* under the pseudonym 'Zambi'. He recorded the song himself, providing all the vocals, and for release as a single the song was split into Part I and Part II.

Surprising Farian, *Baby, Do You Wanna Bump* rose to no.8 in Belgium and no.12 in the Netherlands, prompting him to form a Euro-Caribbean vocal quartet to promote the song. Boney M's original line-up changed several times, before becoming settled: Jamaicans Liz Mitchell and Marcia Barrett, Maizie Williams from Montserrat, and Bobby Farrell, a Dutch man with Aruban ancestry.

For inclusion on the group's debut album, *TAKE THE HEAT OFF ME*, an extended version of the *Baby, Do You Wanna Bump* was created by Farian, by joining together the two parts of the single. This version was also overdubbed with vocals by Liz Mitchell and Marcia Barrett.

Following the huge success of *Rivers Of Babylon* and *Brown Girl In The Ring* in 1987, *Baby, Do You Wanna Bump* was re-issued as a 7" and a limited edition 12" single in the UK, but it wasn't a hit.

2 ~ DADDY COOL

Germany: Hansa 16 959 AT (1976), MCI 74321 69177 2 ('99 Remix, 1999).
  B-side (1976): *No Woman, No Cry.*
  Tracks (1999): *Daddy Cool '99 (Radio Edit)/(Extended Vocal Club Mix)/(Latino Club Mix)/(Solid Disco Edit)/(Original Mix 1976).*

19.07.76: 40-x-42-35-17-9-3-3-**1**-**2**-**1**-**1**-**1**-**1**-**1**-**1**-**1**-**1**-**1**-2-1-4-4-4-8-9-14-15-16-14-24-19-32-49
16.08.99: 54-62-47-61-49-60-53-57-54 ('99 Remix)

UK: Hansa/Atlantic K 10827 (1976), BMG 74321 913 512 (Remix, 2001).
  B-side (1976): *No Woman, No Cry.*
  Tracks (2001): *Daddy Cool 2001 (Jewels & Stone Radio Edit)/(Original Mix)/(Jewels & Stone Club Mix).*

18.12.76: 49-31-31-36-23-18-8-**6**-7-9-13-21-27
29.12.01: 47-58 (2001 Remix)

Australia
24.01.77: peaked at no.**5**, charted for 23 weeks

Austria
15.09.76: 13-4-**1**-**1**-**1**-**1**-6 (monthly chart)

29

DADDY COOL

Words and Music by FARIAN/REYAM

Recorded on ATLANTIC Records by

BONEY M

30p

EDITIONS INTRO/FAR MUSIKVERLAG/HANSA MUSIC/ATV MUSIC LTD
MUSIC SALES LTD • 78 Newman Street • London W1

Belgium (Flanders)
9.10.76: 9-3-2-**1-1-1-1**-2-4-8-14-21

Canada
24.08.77: peaked at no.**42**, charted for 4 weeks

France
2.09.76: peaked at no.**1** (5 weeks), charted for 21 weeks
28.08.99: 42-23-18-16-18-20-23-31-45-43-51-58-56-77-81-x-x-x-99 ('99 Remix)

Netherlands
18.09.15: 28-24-14-11-6-**3-3-3-3**-7-12-24

New Zealand
20.03.77: 18-17-25-**15**-35-18-35-x-x-19-31

Norway
13.11.76: 6-7-5-4-4-4-5-3-3-3-**1-1-1-1-1-1-1-1-1-1**-2-2-2-3-3-3-5-5-5-6-6-7-10-9-9-10

South Africa
20.11.76: peaked at no.**2**, charted for 19 weeks

Spain
21.02.77: peaked at no.**1** (for 7 weeks), charted for 23 weeks

Sweden
2.11.76: 7-3-**1-1-1-1-1-1-1**-2-2-2-2-3-7-5-10-10-16-18
19.08.99: 34-23-19-21-24-23-24-26-28-33-34-39-54-49 ('99 Remix)

Switzerland
1.10.76: 11-4-**1-1-1-1-1-1-1-1-1-1-1-1-1**-2-8-10-12-13-15
5.09.99: 50-49 ('99 Remix)
9.01.00: 94-x-97 ('99 Remix)

USA
22.01.77: 87-75-**65-65-65**

Zimbabwe
8.01.77: peaked at no.**2**, charted for 17 weeks

Daddy Cool was written by Frank Farian and George Reyam, and was the first song Boney M. recorded for their debut album, *TAKE THE HEAT OFF ME*.

Originally, Hansa Records wanted to release Boney M.'s cover of Bob Marley's *No Woman, No Cry* as the follow-up to *Baby, Do You Wanna Bump*. Frank Farian disagreed and, based on reaction to both recordings at his discotheque at St. Ingbert, Germany, he persuaded Hansa to make *Daddy Cool* the A-side instead, which proved to be a smart move.

Daddy Cool was hugely successful in continental Europe especially, topping the chart for four months in Austria, 14 weeks in Switzerland, 12 weeks in Germany, 10 weeks in Norway, and seven weeks in Spain and Sweden. *Daddy Cool* also hit no.1 in Belgium and France, and charted at no.2 in South Africa and Zimbabwe, no.3 in the Netherlands, no.5 in Australia, no.6 in the UK, no.15 in New Zealand and no.42 in Canada. Although only a minor hit, *Daddy Cool* did give Boney M. their first Hot 100 success in the USA.

In 1986, Boney M. celebrated their 10th anniversary with a TV special and a new compilation album, *32 SUPERHITS – THE BEST OF 10 YEARS*. The group planned to release a new single, a cover of 10cc's *Dreadlock Holiday*, from their eighth and final studio album, *EYE DANCE*, as well but this was cancelled in favour of a new version of *Daddy Cool*, to which Frank Farian added rap vocals. This version of *Daddy Cool* wasn't a hit anywhere.

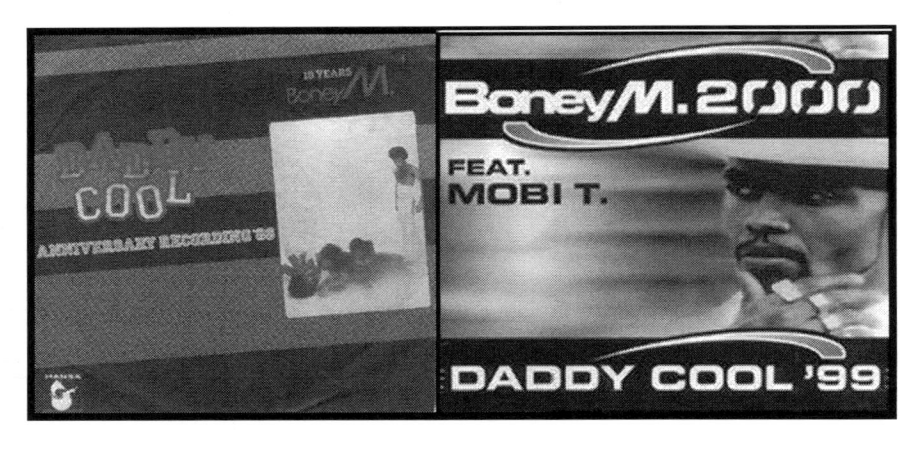

The success of the Sash! and Horny United's remixes of *Ma Baker* prompted Frank Farian to remix *Daddy Cool* in 1999, as the follow-up. The remix was credited to 'Boney M. 2000', and an all new line-up featuring three girls and the rapper Mobi T appeared in the accompanying video. Fans of Boney M. were not impressed, and Frank subsequently dropped plans for the new quartet to front a Boney M. remix album.

The 1999 remix charted at no.16 in France, no.19 in Sweden, no.47 in Germany and no.49 in Switzerland.

Daddy Cool was remixed again in 2001, by Jewels & Stone, for the UK compilation album, *THE GREATEST HITS* ~ as a single, it charted at no.47.

3 ~ SUNNY

Germany: Hansa 17 459 AT (1976).
  B-side: *New York City*.

6.12.76: 36-26-11-6-3-2-2-**1**-**1**-2-2-2-2-2-2-2-9-5-15-16-25-36-21-38-24-48-42

UK: Hansa/Atlantic K 10892 (1977).
  B-side: *New York City*.

12.03.77: 48-22-15-7-9-**3**-8-10-27-30

Australia
16.05.77: peaked at no.**36**, charted for 13 weeks

Austria
15.01.77: 12-2-**1**-6-2 (monthly chart)

Belgium (Flanders)
1.01.77: 11-7-5-2-2-**1**-**1**-2-3-6-12-23

France
18.02.77: peaked at no.**1** (for 2 weeks), charted for 20 weeks
22.01.00: 61-57-56-72-99-99 (Boney M.2000)

Sunny
Recorded on ATLANTIC by
Boney M
CAMPBELL, CONNELLY & Co LTD.
E

Ireland
20.04.77: 17-16-12-8-5-**4-4**-8-10-18

Japan
25.06.77: peaked at no.**41**, charted for 40 weeks

Netherlands
1.01.77: 17-9-4-2-**1-1**-3-8-21

New Zealand
19.06.77: 37-36-x-23-39-**17**-25-26-24-37-36-x-21-19-26-27-x-28-18-31-30-30-39

Norway
22.01.77: 9-x-10-**4**-7-**4-4**-5-5-6-7-7-5-5-6-7-7-7-10-10

Spain
15.08.77: peaked at no.**5**, charted for 16 weeks

Sweden
11.03.77: **11**-14-12-16-14-16

Switzerland
8.01.77: 12-5-5-**2**-4-4-5-5-8-9-12-12
27.02.00: 80 (Boney M.2000)

Sunny was written and originally recorded by Bobby Hebb in 1966. He was inspired to write the song following the murder of his older brother Harold, who was stabbed to death outside a nightclub in Nashville ~ on the same day President John F. Kennedy was assassinated.

'All my intentions were to think of happier times and pay tribute to my brother,' said Hebb, 'basically looking for a brighter day, because times were low. After I wrote it, I thought *Sunny* just might be a different approach to what Johnny Bragg was talking about in *Just Walkin' In The Rain*.'

Hebb's original version of *Sunny* rose to no.2 on the Hot 100 in the USA.

Cher, who was married to Sonny Bono at the time, also recorded a version of *Sunny* in 1966, for her third, self-titled album. Released as a single, her version hit no.1 in Norway, and was a Top 3 hit in Canada, the Netherlands and the USA.

Boney M., with Liz Mitchell singing lead vocals, recorded *Sunny* for their debut album, *TAKE THE HEAT OFF ME*. Released as the follow-up to *Daddy Cool*, *Sunny* hit no.1 in Austria, Belgium, France, Germany and the Netherlands, and achieved no.2 in Switzerland, no.3 in the UK, no.4 in Ireland and Norway, no.5 in Spain, no.11 in Sweden, no.17 in New Zealand, no.36 in Australia and no.41 in Japan.

Like *Daddy Cool*, *Sunny* was remixed in 1999, for the 'Boney M.2000' remix album, *20th CENTURY HITS*, and as a single it was a minor hit in France and Switzerland.

Maizie Williams recorded a solo version of *Sunny* in 2006, but it wasn't a hit.

4 ~ MA BAKER

Germany: Hansa 17 888 AT (1977), Laustark 74321 63942 2 (Remixes, 1999).
  B-side (1977): *Still I'm Sad*.
  Tracks (1999): *Ma Baker (Tokapi Radio Edit)/(Original Edit)/(Extended Vocal Edit)/
    (Disco Dub Edit)*

16.05.77: 37-15-8-3-**1-1-1**-2-2-2-2-2-2-2-2-6-7-11-11-14-16-18-23-25-28-34-42-43
1.02.99: 38-40-34-36-31-28-34-31-36-37-51-43-48-53-70 (Boney M. Vs Sash!)

UK: Hansa/Atlantic K 10965 (1977), Logic 74321 65387 2 (Remixes, 1999).
  B-side (1977): *Still I'm Sad*.
  Tracks (1999): *Somebody Scream (Radio Edit)/Ma Baker (Sash! Radio Edit)/
    (Somebody Scream (Massive Club Mix)/(Ma Baker (Sash! 12" Mix)*

25.06.77: 38-14-5-4-3-**2**-3-5-7-11-19-24-34
8.05.99: 22-46-83 *(Ma Baker/Somebody Scream)*

Australia
8.08.77: peaked at no.**5**, charted for 22 weeks

Austria
15.06.77: 11-**1-1**-3-6-7 (monthly chart)
28.02.99: 34-31-21-19-21-19-22-19-20-19-27-32 (Boney M. Vs Sash!)

MA BAKER

TEXT UND MUSIK: FRANK FARIAN / FRED JAY / REYAM

Klavierausgabe mit Akk.-Bez. Arr.: St. Klinkhammer

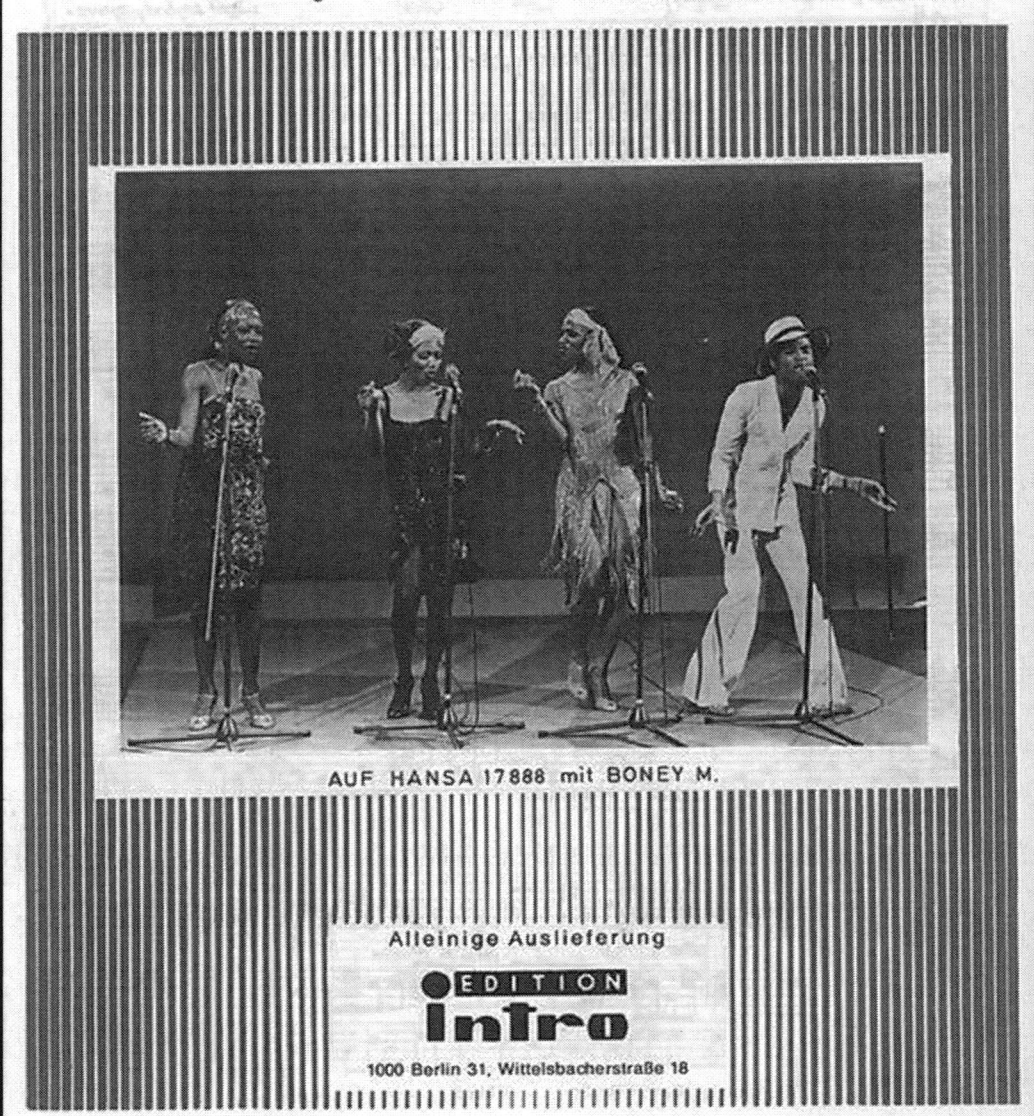

AUF HANSA 17888 mit BONEY M.

Alleinige Auslieferung

EDITION intro

1000 Berlin 31, Wittelsbacherstraße 18

Belgium (Flanders)
28.05.78: 16-5-2-**1-1-1-1-1-1**-2-3-4-10-13-24
13.02.99: 32-27-30-27-24-26-27-29-33-46 (Boney M. Vs Sash!)

Canada
25.01.78: peaked at no.**38**, charted for 8 weeks

Finland
16.01.99: **6-6** (Boney M. Vs Sash!)

France
1.07.77: peaked at no.**1** (for 4 weeks), charted for 27 weeks
24.04.99: 29-14-11-13-14-14-15-17-20-21-23-29-28-34-45-46-51-50-62-63-67-73-65-77
('99 Remix)

Ireland
27.07.77: 18-11-6-5-6-**4**

Japan
25.10.77: peaked at no.**72**, charted for 14 weeks

Netherlands
21.05.77: 24-8-3-**1-1-1-1-1-1**-3-4-8-18-30
6.02.99: 58-41-34-35-39-49-50-70-91 (Boney M. Vs Sash!)

New Zealand
25.09.77: 36-31-39-13-**2**-3-**2**-3-3-4-4-7-9-9-9-9-9-25-35
28.02.99: 22-15-9-20-27-24-21-28-33 *(Ma Baker/Somebody Scream)*

Norway
28.05.77: 4-4-3-**1-1**-3-2-**1-1-1-1-1-1-1**-2-2-2-2-3-3-4-4-5

South Africa
6.08.77: peaked at no.**2**, charted for 13 weeks

Spain
19.12.77: peaked at no.**1** (for 1 week), charted for 26 weeks
27.12.99: peaked at no.**10**, charted for 4 weeks ('99 Remix)

Sweden
20.05.77: 10-4-3-3-**1-1-1**-2-3-6-8-14-18
11.03.99: 16-11-10-11-11-13-12-16-19-27-32-39-40 (Boney M. Vs Sash!)

Switzerland
28.05.77: 15-8-3-**1-1-1**-3-3-3-3-3-4-6-8-8-10-11-15
7.02.99: 24-32-21-24-24-35-31-28-28-25-29-37-38-50-38-x-42-x-43 (Boney M. Vs Sash!)

USA
27.08.77: **96-96**-100

Zimbabwe
20.08.77: peaked at no.1 (for 4 weeks), charted for 18 weeks

Ma Baker was based on the Tunisian folk song, *Sidi Mansour*, which Frank Farian's assistant Hans-Jörg Mayer discovered whilst on holiday, and re-wrote as a disco track.

The lyrics, penned by Fred Jay, were inspired by the 1930s outlaw Kate 'Ma' Barker, who was the mother of several gangsters who ran the notorious Barker gang. Ma Barker, who travelled with the gang, was killed in a shoot-out with the FBI in Ocklawaha, Florida, on 16th January 1936; her son Fred was killed in the same shoot-out.

'Barker didn't rhyme too well so it was changed to Baker,' said Marcia Barrett. 'Apparently she hid her sons from the cops before getting involved in a web of crime herself. Any mother would go to great lengths to protect her children, and apparently she met a violent end, just like the song says.'

Boney M. recorded *Ma Baker* for their second album, *LOVE FOR SALE*, with Linda Blake voicing Ma Baker on the recording. The track was chosen as the lead single. It maintained the group's run of success, topping the chart in Norway for nine weeks, in Austria for eight weeks, and in Belgium and the Netherlands for six weeks. Ma Baker also hit no.1 in Germany, France, Spain, Sweden, Switzerland and Zimbabwe.

Ma Baker gave Boney M. their biggest hit to date in the UK, where it peaked at no.2, behind Donna Summer's *I Feel Love*. The single also charted at no.2 in New Zealand and

South Africa, no.4 in Ireland and no.5 in Australia, but it was only a minor hit in Canada, Japan and the USA.

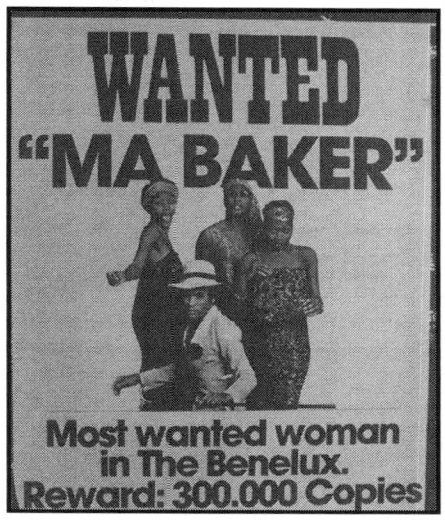

Following the success of a remix of *Brown Girl In The Ring* in 1993, Frank Farian tried his luck with *Ma Baker*, but it wasn't successful and failed to chart anywhere. The remix was included on the 1993 compilation, *MORE GOLD – 20 SUPER HITS VOL. II*.

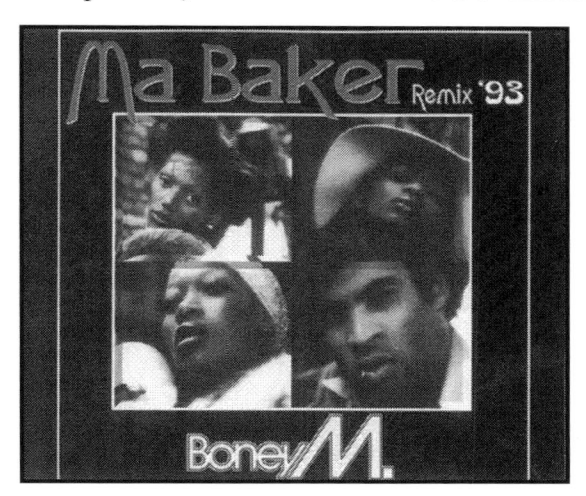

In late 1998, a Sash! remix of *Ma Baker* was released as a 12" single ~ however, before it was issued on CD, it was withdrawn, and a *Ma Baker/Somebody Scream* remix featuring Horny United released instead.

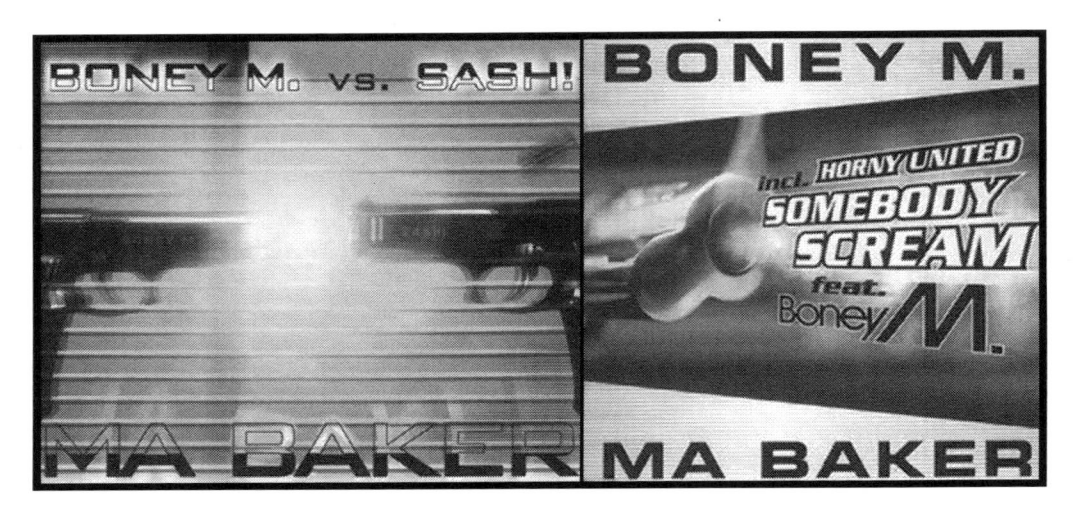

The various Sash! / Horny United remixes of *Ma Baker* charted at no.6 in Finland, no.9 in New Zealand, no.10 in Spain and Sweden, no.11 in France, no.19 in Austria, no.21 in Switzerland, no.22 in the UK, no.24 in Belgium, no.28 in Germany and no.34 in the Netherlands.

5 ~ STILL I'M SAD

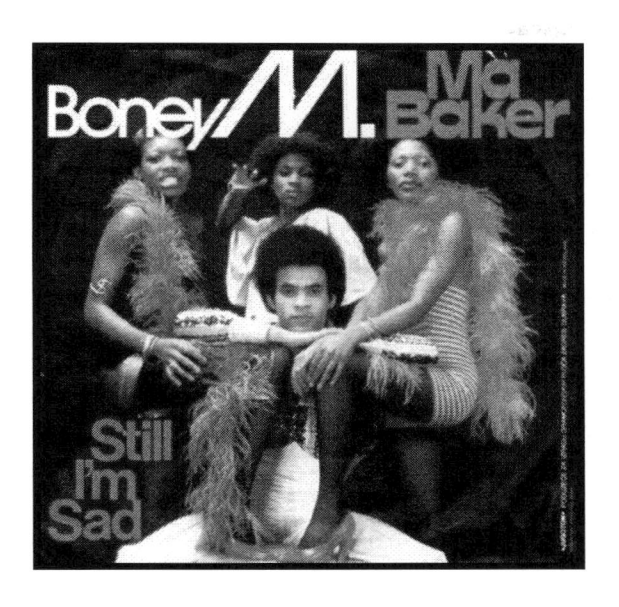

Still I'm Sad was released as the B-side of *Ma Baker* in Germany and the UK.

Sweden
20.05.77: **17**

Still I'm Sad was written by Jim McCarty and Paul Samwell-Smith, and was originally recorded by The Yardbirds for their 1965 album, *HAVING A RAVE UP WITH THE YARDBIRDS* ~ the following year, it featured as the lead song on a four track EP issued in France.

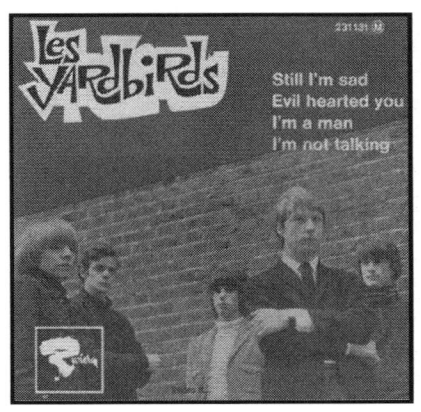

Boney M. recorded *Still I'm Sad* for their second album, *LOVE FOR SALE*. In most countries, it was released as the B-side of *Ma Baker*, but it charted in its own right in Sweden, spending a solitary week on the chart at no.17.

6 ~ GENTLEMEN CALLERS NOT ALLOWED

Netherlands: Hansa 11 315 AT (1977).
  B-side: *Say Yes* (Gilla).

13.08.77: 30-28-19-**15**-17

Gentlemen Callers Not Allowed was written by Frank Farian and Fred Jay, and was recorded by Bobby Farrell with Austrian singer Gisela 'Gilla' Wuchinger.
  Somewhat ironically, given he made no vocal contribution to Boney M. recordings, Bobby was the first – and what proved to be the only – member of Boney M. to achieve a Top 40 hit single outside the group.
  Gentlemen Callers Not Allowed was only released in the Netherlands, where it rose to no.15, during a five week chart run.

7 ~ BELFAST

Germany: Hansa 11 537 AT (1977).
B-side: *Plantation Boy*.

3.10.77: 29-40-5-**1-1-1-1**-2-4-5-6-8-10-11-11-10-17-20-29-31-30-44-48-x-x-x-49-48-x-47-x-x-x-45

UK: Hansa/Atlantic K 11020 (1977).
B-side: *Plantation Boy*.

29.10.77: 47-34-22-21-17-19-10-**8**-11-11-12-21-30

Australia
19.12.77: peaked at no.**57**, charted for 12 weeks

Austria
15.11.77: 6-3-4-**2**-25 (monthly chart)

Belgium (Flanders)
8.10.77: 26-14-9-4-3-3-**1**-2-2-3-9-14-19-24

France
6.01.78: peaked at no.**1** (for 3 weeks), charted for 22 weeks

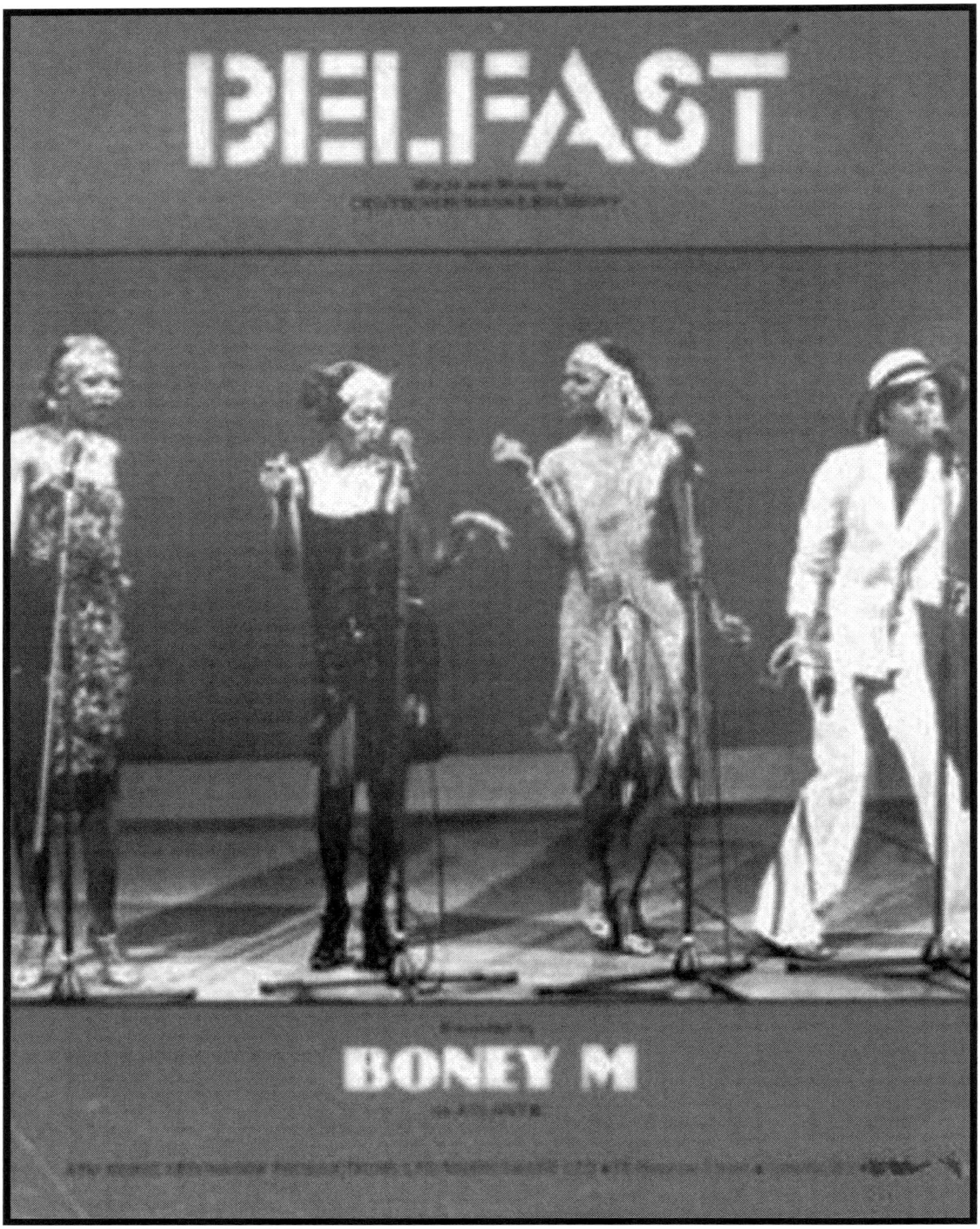
BELFAST
BONEY M

Ireland
9.11.77: 18-3-**1**-2-5-5-6-12

Japan
25.02.78: peaked at no.**85**, charted for 7 weeks

Netherlands
15.10.77: 18-6-**3-3-3-3**-4-7-10-14-21

Spain
20.03.78: peaked at no.**3**, charted for 16 weeks

Switzerland
22.10.77: 13-8-3-3-**1-1-1-1-1-1-1-1-1-1**-3-8-11-13-14

Zimbabwe
7.01.78: peaked at no.**12**, charted for 4 weeks

Originally titled 'Londonderry', and inspired by the troubles in Northern Ireland, Drafi Deutscher wrote *Belfast* in the early 1970s for Marcia Barrett, in her pre-Boney M. days when she was still a solo artist.

As they didn't yet have enough songs of their own, Boney M. performed *Belfast* in concert regularly in the early days, and the crowd reaction was invariably favourable. When this was brought to his attention, Frank Farian decided to record the song – with Marcia singing lead vocals – for Boney M.'s second album, *LOVE FOR SALE*.

Belfast was chosen as the follow-up to *Ma Baker* and, while it couldn't match its success, it was still a sizeable hit. The single topped the chart in Switzerland for 10 straight weeks, and gave Boney M. their fourth consecutive no.1 in Germany. *Belfast* also achieved no.1 in Belgium, France and Ireland, no.2 in Austria, no.3 in the Netherlands and Spain, no.8 in the UK and no.12 in Zimbabwe, but it was only a minor hit in Australia and Japan.

In North America, due to the political context of the song, *Belfast* was omitted from the *LOVE FOR SALE* album, and replaced with *Daddy Cool*.

Marcia Barrett recorded a solo version of *Belfast* for her 2005 album, *COME INTO MY LIFE*, but it wasn't released as a single.

8 ~ RIVERS OF BABYLON / BROWN GIRL IN THE RING

Germany: Hansa 11 999 AT (1978).
    Hansa 111 825 (*Rivers Of Babylon Remix '88*) (1988).
      B-side: *Mary's Boy Child / Oh My Lord (Remix '88)*.
    MCI 74321 13705 7 (*Brown Girl In The Ring '93 Remix*) (1993).
      B-side: *Brown Girl In The Ring (Radio Rap Version)*.

17.04.78: 2-**1-1-1-1-1-1-1-1-1-1-1-1-1-1-1**-2-1-3-2-4-5-12-14-19-24-23-31-30-29-27-30-41-45-46-50

UK: Hansa/Atlantic K 11120 (1978).
    Hansa 111 825 (*Rivers Of Babylon Remix '88*) (1988).
      B-side: *Mary's Boy Child / Oh My Lord (Remix '88)*.
    MCI 74321 13705 7 (*Brown Girl In The Ring '93 Remix*) (1993).
      B-side: *Brown Girl In The Ring (Radio Rap Version)*.

29.04.78: 21-2-**1-1-1-1-1**-2-3-6-10-18-20-18-10-6-5-4-3-2-3-5-10-21-28-37-45-52-65-71-71-75-74-62-57-57-44-53-70-65
17.04.93: 38-47-75 (*Brown Girl In The Ring '93 Remix*)

Australia
5.06.78: peaked at no.**1** (for 6 weeks), charted for 24 weeks

Austria
15.05.78: **1-1-1-1**-4-7-11 (monthly chart)

Belgium (Flanders)
15.04.78: 16-5-**1-1-1-1-1-1-1-1-1-1-1**-3-4-12-22
22.05.93: 46 (*Brown Girl In The Ring '93 Remix*)

Canada
6.09.78: peaked at no.**8**, charted for 32 weeks (*Rivers Of Babylon*)
8.08.79: peaked at no.47, charted for 4 weeks (*Brown Girl In The Ring*)

France
21.04.78: peaked at no.**1** (for 4 weeks), charted for 25 weeks

Ireland
11.05.78: 13-2-**1-1-1-1**-5-x-2-4-4-3-29-14-4-4-2-3-3-2-6-7-9-13-18-22-25-26-28-25-30
26.01.79: 29-28-27
25.04.93: 25 (*Brown Girl In The Ring '93 Remix*)

Japan
25.05.78: peaked at no.**60**, charted for 21 weeks

Netherlands
15.04.78: 17-**1-1-1-1-1-1-1-1-1-1-1**-2-2-4-4-9-13-20-23-27-38
8.01.11: 70

New Zealand
25.06.78: 26-2-**1-1-1-1-1-1-1-1-1-1-1-1-1-1**-2-5-15-18-15-9-13-17-17-25-25-25-25-25-31-39
9.04.89: 46 (*Rivers Of Babylon '88 Remix*)
8.04.96: 36-30-36-23-23-32-20-28-29-38-39 (*Brown Girl In The Ring '93 Remix*)

Norway
6.05.78: 10-10-8-8-x-x-x-6-3-**1-1-1-1-1-1**-2-2-2-2-2-2-2-2-2-4-6-4-4-6-10-9

South Africa
10.06.78: peaked at no.**1** (for 11 weeks), charted for 21 weeks

Spain
28.08.78: peaked at no.**1** (for 5 weeks), charted for 27 weeks

Sweden
5.05.78: 13-9-6-**1-1-1-1-1**-5-4-5-10-11-16

Switzerland
8.04.78: 4-**1-1-1-1-1-1-1-1-1-1-1-1-1**-2-4-7-11-12-15

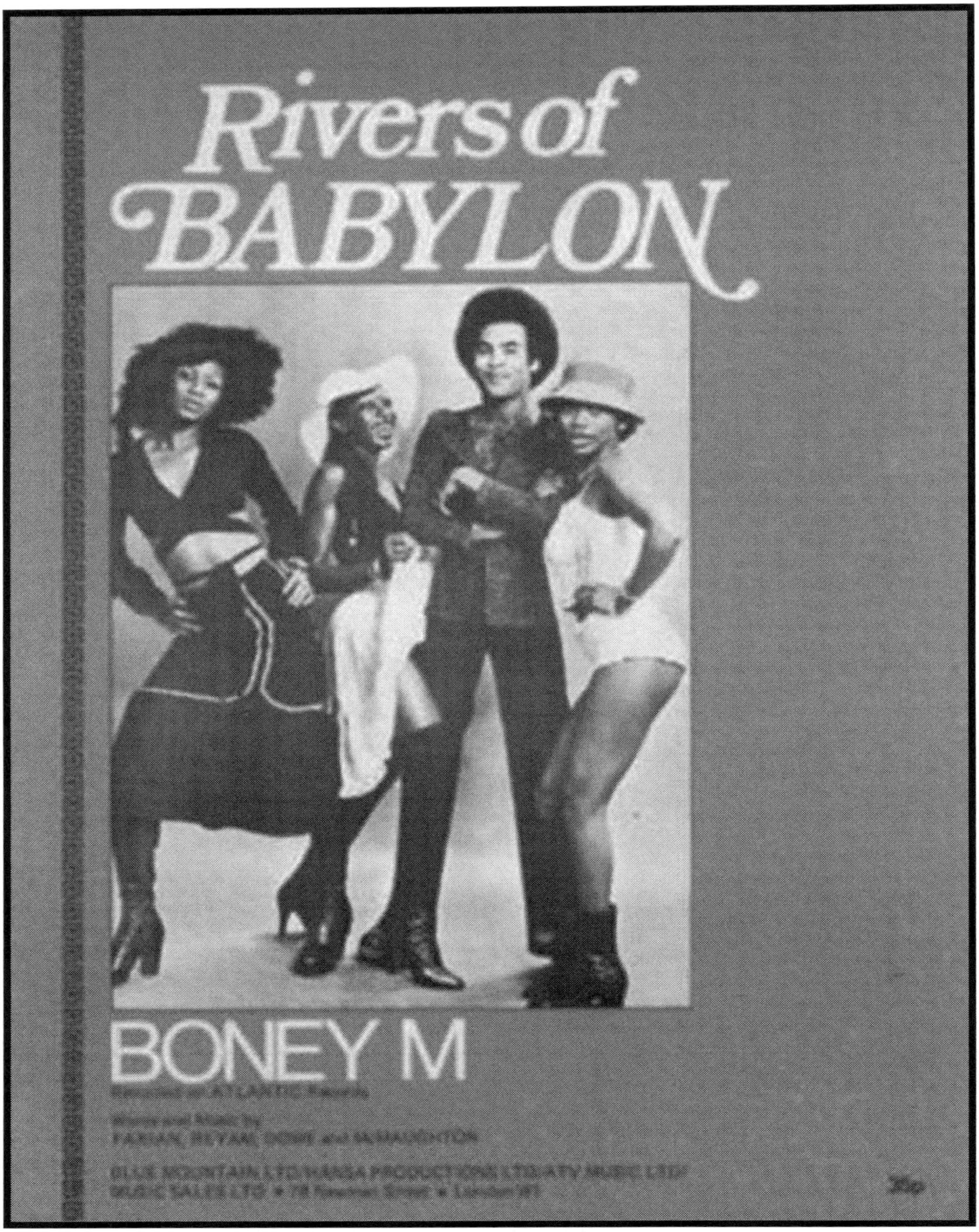
Rivers of
BABYLON
BONEY M

USA
3.06.78: 87-76-66-56-48-46-44-39-37-35-33-31-**30**-49-69-69-100

Zimbabwe
17.06.78: peaked at no.**1** (for 10 weeks), charted for 26 weeks
19.03.94: peaked at no.**1** (for 1 week), charted for 7 weeks (*Brown Girl In The Ring '93 Remix*)

Rivers Of Babylon was written by Brent Dowe and Trevor McNaughton, and started life as a Rastafari song that was originally recorded by the Jamaican reggae group The Melodians in 1970. The song's lyrics were adapted from Psalms 19 and 137 of the Hebrew Bible.

In the Rastafarian faith, the term 'Babylon' relates to a government that is unjust or oppressive, and in writing the song Dowe wanted to increase the public's consciousness of the growing Rastafarian movement, and its calls for black liberation and social justice. Initially, this led to the song being banned by the Jamaican government, but that didn't stop *Rivers Of Babylon* from going to no.1 on the island's chart.

Rivers Of Babylon found a wider audience in 1972, when it featured on the soundtrack to the film, *The Harder They Come*.

With a few changes to the lyrics, Boney M. recorded *Rivers Of Babylon* for their third album, *NIGHTFLIGHT TO VENUS*. The track was released as the album's lead single and, initially, Frank Farian and Reyam (*aka* Hans-Jörg Mayer) were credited as the song's only composers. However, subsequent pressings did acknowledge Brent Dowe and Trevor McNaughton as co-composers.

'*Rivers Of Babylon* is the sort of song my mother would have wanted me to sing,' said Marcia Barrett, 'although I never would have believed her at the time. It's the sort of song that makes people who don't normally buy singles go and get a copy. You know, the sort of people who've only got five records in the house!'

Rivers Of Babylon was hugely successful, topping the chart in Germany for 17 weeks, and giving Boney M. their fifth consecutive no.1 single. The single spent 16 weeks at no.1

in Austria, 14 weeks at no.1 in New Zealand and Switzerland, 11 weeks at no.1 in Belgium, the Netherlands and South Africa, and 10 weeks at no.1 in Zimbabwe.

Rivers Of Babylon was the first Boney M. single to go to no.1 in the UK, where it stayed for five weeks, and went on to sell more than two million copies, making it – at the time – the UK's no.2 best-selling single of all-time, after *Mull Of Kintyre* by Wings. The single also hit no.1 in Australia, France, Ireland, Norway, Spain and Sweden, and achieved no.8 in Canada and no.30 in the USA.

Originally, *Rivers Of Babylon* was released with Boney M.'s version of *Brown Girl In The Ring* on the B-side.

'It's a hundred-year-old Jamaican children's song,' Marcia Barrett wrote in her autobiography, *Forward – My Life With & Without Boney M.*, 'and we would dance around in a circle, holding hands and singing, with one of us in the middle.'

The line 'Show me your motion' meant the girl in the middle had to show her best dance moves, while 'Skip across the ocean' meant the girl in the middle picked a partner to dance with, and then that child would stay in the middle and become the next 'brown girl in the ring'.

Liz Mitchell had previously recorded *Brown Girl In The Ring*, as *Brown Girl*, in 1975 with Malcolm's Locks.

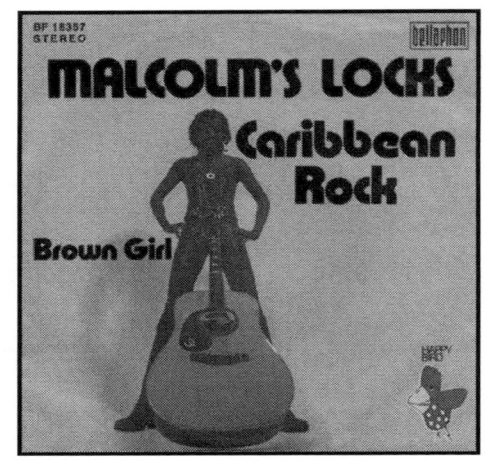

Rivers Of Babylon was slipping down the charts in most countries when *Brown Girl In The Ring* started picking up airplay, leading to its promotion to a double A-side in many countries. This helped to extend the single's chart life, something that was especially noticeable in Ireland and the UK, where the single rebounded from no.29 to no.2 and from no.20 to no.2, respectively.

The members of Boney M. went their separate ways, following their 10th anniversary concert, but marked their reunion in 1988 with a remixed version of *Rivers Of Babylon*. The single achieved no.46 in New Zealand, but wasn't a hit in most countries.

BROWN GIRL IN THE RING
Traditional arranged by
FRANK FARIAN and STEFAN KLINKHAMMER
Recorded on ATLANTIC by
BONEY M
FAR MUSIKVERLAG/HANSA PRODUCTIONS LTD/ATV MUSIC LTD/MUSIC SALES LTD
78 Newman Street • London W1
35p

Five years later, Frank Farian remixed *Brown Girl In The Ring*, with new lead vocals by Liz Mitchell. This remix enjoyed more success, hitting no.1 in Zimbabwe and charting at no.23 in New Zealand, no.25 in Ireland, no.38 in the UK and no.46 in Belgium.

'Both *Rivers Of Babylon* and *Brown Girl In The Ring* are original songs from Jamaica,' said Liz Mitchell, looking back on their success. 'The messages in the songs are people friendly, they speak of the distress we suffer and the joy we have in listening to the rhythms of the Caribbean. It was just wonderful as these songs were received by our audiences around the world.'

In 1978, The Barron Knights released *A Taste Of Aggro* ~ a parody of *Rivers Of Babylon*, *The Smurf Song* and Brian & Michael's *Matchstick Men And Matchstick Cats And Dogs*. The single peaked at no.3 in the UK, making it the group's most successful single.

9 ~ RASPUTIN

Germany: Hansa 15 808 AT (1978).
  B-side: *Painter Man*.

4.09.78: 49-16-2-2-2-**1**-4-3-3-4-7-7-13-20-21-24-33-37-26-48

UK: Hansa/Atlantic K 11192 (1978).
  B-side: *Never Change Lovers In The Middle Of The Night*.

7.10.78: 9-3-**2-2**-4-7-11-22-41-52
4.03.89: 100

Australia
16.10.78: peaked at no.**1** (for 2 weeks), charted for 23 weeks

Austria
15.10.78: 2-**1**-3-16 (monthly chart)

Belgium (Flanders)
9.09.78: 14-8-4-2-2-**1**-2-3-4-10-14-23-23-27 (b/w *Painter Man*)

Canada
21.02.79: peaked at no.**6**, charted for 28 weeks

France
4.08.78: peaked at no.**2**, charted for 28 weeks

Ireland
6.10.78: 6-4-**3**-4-5-5-7-8-15

Japan
25.10.78: peaked at no.**26**, charted for 29 weeks

Netherlands
16.09.78: 19-6-10-87-7-**5**-11-25-33-43 *(b/w Painter Man)*

New Zealand
5.11.78: 12-12-8-6-**4-4**-8-8-8-8-8-13-16-15-33-40

Norway
4.11.78: **10-10-10**

South Africa
23.09.78: peaked at no.**9**, charted for 7 weeks

Spain
27.11.78: peaked at no.**3**, charted for 18 weeks

Switzerland
16.09.78: 12-4-**2-2**-4-4-5-7-8-10-14

Zimbabwe
30.09.78: peaked at no.**6**, charted for 13 weeks

Written by Frank Farian, Fred Jay and George Reyam, *Rasputin* was inspired by the life of the early 20th century Russian mystic and preacher, Grigori Rasputin. Rasputin was an associate and advisor to the family of Russia's last monarch, Tsar Nicholas II; Nicholas, his wife Alexandra and their five children were brutally executed by their Bolshevik guards on the night of 16th-17th July 1918.

In the song, Rasputin is portrayed as 'Russia's greatest love machine'. After surviving poisoned wine, *Rasputin* climaxes with 'and so they shot him 'til he was dead … oh, those Russians!'. In real life, Grigori Rasputin was murdered on the morning of 30th December 1916 ~ he died of three gunshot wounds, including one point-blank shot to his forehead.

Rasputin was released as the second single from *NIGHTFLIGHT TO VENUS*, and continued Boney M.'s run of success. It hit no.1 in Australia, Austria, Belgium and Germany, and charted at no.2 in France, Switzerland and the UK, no.3 in Ireland and Spain, no.4 in New Zealand, no.5 in the Netherlands, no.6 in Canada and Zimbabwe, no.9 in South Africa, no.10 in Norway and no.26 in Japan.

Rasputin

Words and Music by
FARIAN, REYAM, and JAY

Recorded on ATLANTIC Records by
Boney M.

In Belgium and the Netherlands the single's B-side, *Painter Man*, was listed alongside *Rasputin* on the chart.

Rasputin was omitted from Russian pressings of NIGHTFLIGHT TO VENUS, but this didn't stop Boney M. from becoming the first Western pop band to be invited to perform in the Soviet Union. However, for their ten concerts in Moscow in December 1978, the group were barred from performing *Rasputin*.

BONEY M WOW THE RUSSIANS

BONEY M, still number one in the charts with 'Mary's Boy Child', are back in Germany after a triumphant visit to Russia.

The group played in Moscow for ten nights. But Boney M's Liz Mitchell said: "It was exhausting, we played two shows every night — and then we were expected to attend Embassy parties."

But the shows appeared to be a success, with more people outside than watching the concerts — although temperatures were well below freezing.

And on the last night the show was beamed to America live by satellite by the NBC broadcasting network.

Boney M's concerts attracted American journalists who flew into Moscow especially to see them.

The following year, Boney M. appeared at the Sopot Festival in Poland, and again they were asked not to include *Rasputin* in their set-list. This time, however, they defied government officials, and did perform *Rasputin*.

Look-in

YOUR TOP TV FAVOURITES INSIDE!

Junior TVTimes No. 46 week ending 11 November 1978 Every Thursday 10p

BONEY M INTERVIEW & BIG COLOUR PIN-UP ★ WIN THEIR LP!

ON THE BALL ● VINCE HILAIRE

MIND YOUR LANGUAGE

MEET THE SMURFS!

FAMOUS FIVE

THE SIX MILLION DOLLAR MAN ★ **THE BIONIC WOMAN**

HOW THE WEST WAS WON

picture strips

SUPER COMP INSIDE: MANY PRIZES!
see p. 11

10 ~ MARY'S BOY CHILD / OH MY LORD

Germany: Hansa 100 075 (1978), Hansa 111 944 (1988), Hansa 74321 11932 7 (1992).
 B-side 1978): *Dancing In The Streets*.
 A-side (1988): *Rivers Of Babylon (Remix '88)*.
 B-side (1992): *Zion's Daughter*.

11.12.78: 3-2-2-2-**1**-2-2-6-17-21-28-34-46

UK: Hansa/Atlantic K11221 (1978), Ariola 111 947 (1988), Ariola 74321 12512 7 (1992).
 B-side (1978): *Dancing In The Streets*.
 Double A-side (1988): *Mega Mix*.
 A-side (1992): *MegaMix*.

2.12.78: 7-**1**-**1**-**1**-**1**-2-7-32
24.12.88: 55-52-74 *(b/w Mega Mix)*
15.12.07: 83-61-47
3.01.15: 79
2.01.16: 74
15.12.16: 81-77-61-50
14.12.17: 97-48-46-29
13.12.18: 100-75-60-26

Australia
25.12.78: peaked at no.**33**, charted for 12 weeks

Austria
15.01.79: **3-3**-18 (monthly chart)

Belgium (Flanders)
9.12.78: 24-10-**4-4-4**-5-7-11-23-28

Canada
10.01.79: peaked at no.**37**, charted for 4 weeks

Denmark
5.01.79: ***1-1-1**-8-10-10 (* first Danish singles chart)
2.01.15: 38
1.01.16: 16
5.01.18: 32

France
1.12.78: peaked at no.**28**, charted for 11 weeks

Masters of the Megahit

BONEY M: 'Mary's Boy Child' (Atlantic). If this isn't number one within a couple of weeks of release, I'll be greatly surprised. I might even put money on it. This lot have the market so well taped it fair takes my breath away. With the sure footedness of Abba, they've cleaned up this year and the Xmas market is an obvious target. Their delicate harmonies and light Jamaica coating has given this the Midas glow. You'll be sick of it by the time you're hanging up your pillow slip — I guarantee it. A sure sign of a megahit.

Mary's Boy Child

Words and Music by
JESTER HAIRSTON

Recorded on
ATLANTIC/HANSA K 11221
by

Boney M

BOURNE MUSIC LTD · sole selling agents · MUSIC SALES LTD · 78 Newman Street London W1

Ireland
1.12.78: **1-1-1-1-1-1**-2-12-29
24.12.15: 85
28.12.18: 88

Netherlands
16.12.78: **2-2-2-2**-3-10-31
29.12.18: 83

New Zealand
21.01.79: **8**-11-25-34
23.12.79: 46
31.12.18: 29

Norway
16.12.78: 10-4-**2-2-2-2-2**-3-3-4-7-10-10

South Africa
23.12.78: peaked at no.**1** (for 2 weeks), charted for 10 weeks

Spain
25.12.78: peaked at no.**10**, charted for 5 weeks

Sweden
15.12.78: 14-4-**1**-3-7-11
27.12.13: 59
25.12.15: 85

Switzerland
3.12.78: 12-2-**1-1-1-1-1**-2-4-10-14
4.01.09: 98

USA
23.12.78: 90-90-90-86-**85**

Zimbabwe
10.02.79: peaked at no.**5**, charted for 12 weeks

Mary's Boy Child started life as 'He Pone And Chocolate Tea', a song Jester Hairston was asked to write for a birthday party ('pone' is a type of corn bread). This version of the song was never recorded but, when he was asked to write a new Christmas song for Walter Schumann's Hollywood Choir, Hairston remembered his birthday party song, and simply re-wrote the lyrics with a Christmas theme, and re-titled it *Mary's Boy Child*.

Harry Belafonte heard Schumann's Hollywood Choir perform *Mary's Boy Child*, and liked what he heard so much he asked if he could record the song. He did so in 1956, for his album *AN EVENING WITH HARRY BELAFONTE*, which was released the following year. *Mary's Boy Child* was released as a single, and became of the Christmas no.1 of 1957 in the UK, where it went on to become the country's first recognised million selling single.

Boney M. recorded *Mary's Boy Child*, as a non-album single, in November 1978. It was recorded as a medley with *Oh My Lord*, which was composed by Frank Farian and Fred Jay, and rush-released in time for the festive season.

Mary's Boy Child gave Boney M. their seventh straight no.1 single in Germany, and it also topped the charts in Denmark, Ireland, South Africa, Sweden, Switzerland and the UK, where it went on to sell two million copies. Elsewhere, the single achieved no.2 in the Netherlands and Norway, no.3 in Austria, no.4 in Belgium, no.5 in Zimbabwe, no.8 in New Zealand, no.10 in Spain, no.28 in France, no.33 in Australia, no.37 in Canada and no.38 in Denmark.

Mary's Boy Child / Oh My Lord was remixed again in 1992, as the 'Christmas Mega Mix', for inclusion on the album, *THE MOST BEAUTIFUL CHRISTMAS SONGS IN THE WORLD*. Again, the remix was released as a single, backed by *Zion's Daughter* in some countries and as the B-side of *MegaMix* in others. This time, however, the single wasn't a hit anywhere.

RECORD MIRROR

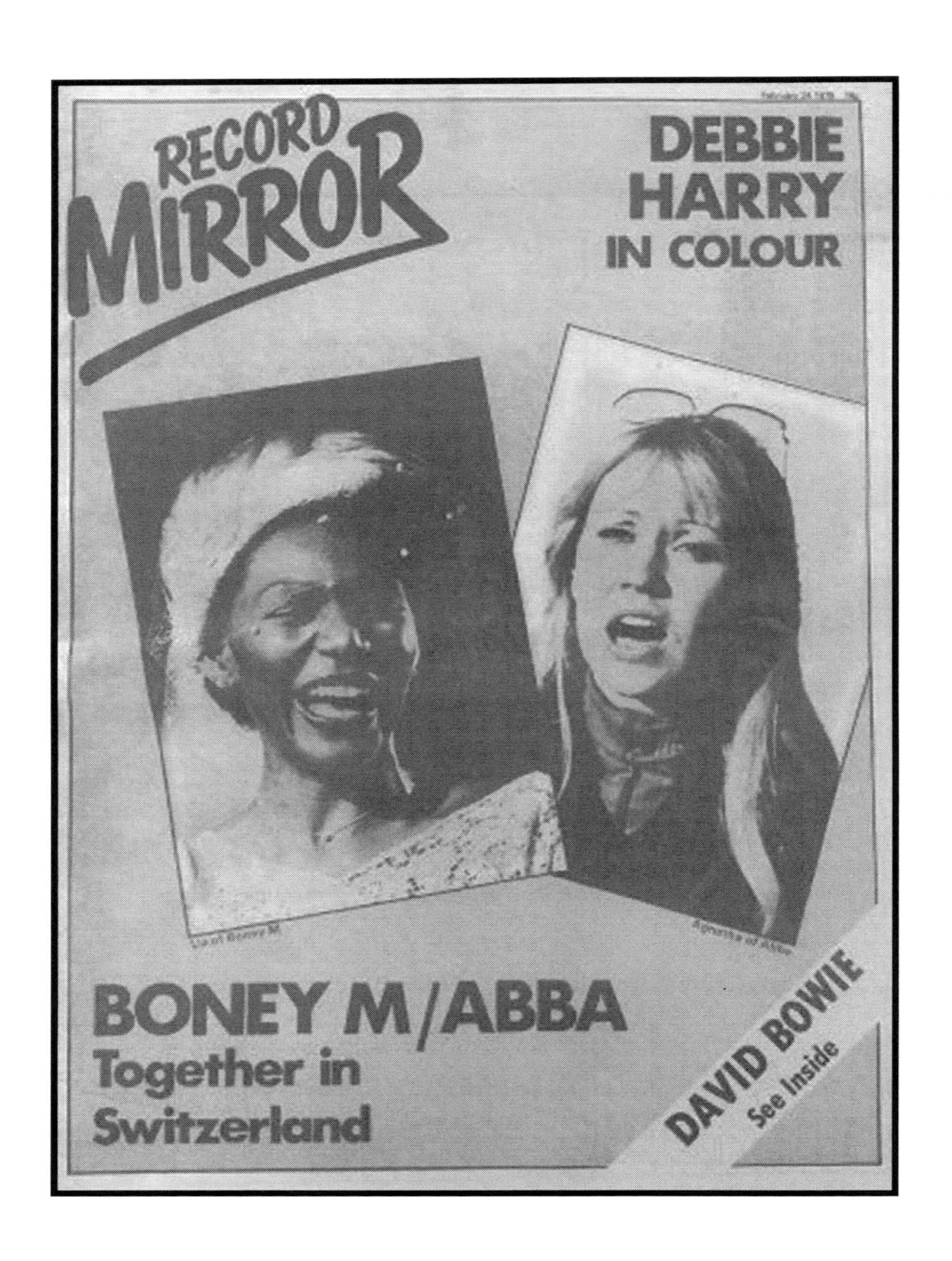

DEBBIE HARRY IN COLOUR

BONEY M/ABBA
Together in Switzerland

DAVID BOWIE See Inside

11 ~ DANCING IN THE STREETS

Germany & UK: released as the B-side of *Mary's Boy Child / Oh My Lord*.

Denmark
2.03.79: **4**
4.05.79: **4**-**4**-8-7

Dancing In The Streets, a Frank Farian composition, was released as the B-side of *Mary's Boy Child / Oh My Lord* in most countries, but was issued as a single in its own right in a few, including Canada, Italy and the USA.

In the USA, *Dancing In The Streets* spent six weeks on the 'bubbling under' the Hot 100, where it peaked at no.3, but it failed to enter the Hot 100. The single did rather better in Denmark, where it achieved three weeks at no.4.

12 ~ PAINTER MAN

Germany: released as the B-side of *Rasputin*.

UK: Hansa/Atlantic K11255 (1979).
  B-side: *He Was A Steppenwolf*.

3.03.79: 26-**10**-11-11-22-59

Belgium (Flanders)
9.09.78: 14-8-4-2-2-**1**-2-3-4-10-14-23-23-27 (b/w *Rasputin*)

Ireland
9.03.79: 22-13-**12**-20-30

Netherlands
16.09.78: 19-6-10-87-7-**5**-11-25-33-43 *(b/w Rasputin)*

Painter Man was written by Kenny Pickett and Eddie Phillips, and was originally recorded by The Creation in 1966 ~ the single was a small hit in the UK, spending two weeks on the chart and peaking at no.36.

PAINTER MAN

Words and Music by K. PICKETT & E. PHILLIPS

Recorded by

Boney M.

on ATLANTIC HANSA Records

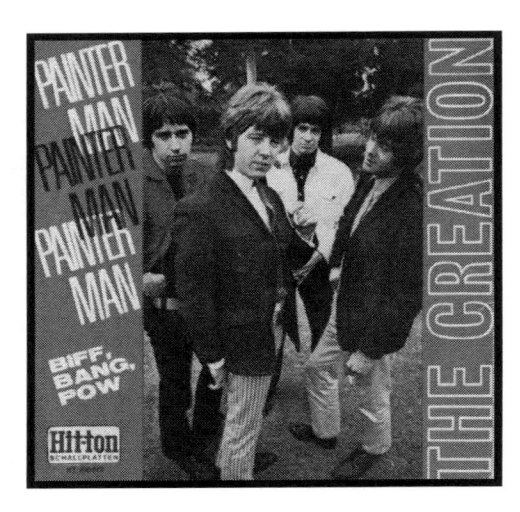

Boney M. recorded *Painter Man* for their 1978 album, *NIGHTFLIGHT TO VENUS*. In most countries, it was released as the B-side of *Rasputin*, and in Belgium and the Netherlands it was listed alongside *Rasputin* on the chart, peaking at no.1 in Belgium and no.5 in the Netherlands.

Painter Man was only released as a single in its own right in a few countries, including the UK and Ireland, and Australasia. The single charted at no.10 in the UK, where it was issued as a limited edition 12" single in translucent red and translucent yellow vinyl, and no.12 in Ireland.

13 ~ HOORAY! HOORAY! IT'S A HOLI-HOLIDAY

Germany: Hansa 100 444 (1979), MCI 74321 71168 2 (1999).
  B-side (1979): *Ribbons Of Blue*.
  Tracks (1999): *Caribbean Night Fever – Megamix (Hooray! Hooray!/Brown Girl In The Ring/No Woman, No Cry/Calendar Song) (Radio Edit)/Hooray! Hooray! It's A Holi-Holiday (Radio Edit)*.

9.04.79: 9-9-**4-4-4-4**-5-6-9-15-15-17-15-17-19-22-27-30-34-47-43-49
22.11.99: 79-95-97 (*Caribbean Night Fever – Megamix*)

UK: Hansa/Atlantic K 11279 (1979).
  B-side: *Ribbons Of Blue*.

28.04.79: 19-4-**3-3**-7-17-29-48-74

Australia
28.05.79: peaked at no.**7**, charted for 18 weeks

Austria
15.05.79: 4-**3**-11-21 (monthly chart)

Belgium (Flanders)
7.04.79: 29-14-9-2-2-2-**1**-4-6-9-15-25

Hooray Hooray It's A Holi-Holiday

BONEY M

Denmark
13.04.79: 4-3-3-**1**-**1**-3-2-9-7-10

France
6.04.79: peaked at no.**14**, charted for 22 weeks

Ireland
4.05.79: 12-**5**-6-10-14-24-25-29

Japan
25.05.79: peaked at no.**31**, charted for 16 weeks

Netherlands
14.04.79: 8-**1**-**1**-**1**-3-2-4-9-15-15-25-33-50

New Zealand
10.06.79: 27-15-16-**7**-10-13-17-22-22-27-38-40-45
13.02.00: 47-x-49 (*Caribbean Night Fever – Megamix*)

Norway
28.04.79: 7-4-4-4-3-3-3-**2**-3-4-5-9

South Africa
26.05.79: peaked at no.**12**, charted for 10 weeks

Spain
23.07.79: peaked at no.**6**, charted for 12 weeks
29.11.99: peaked at no.**6**, charted for 8 weeks (*Caribbean Night Fever – Megamix*)

Sweden
20.04.79: 18-15-**11**-15-14

Switzerland
1.04.79: 15-5-**4**-5-**4**-**4**-7-9-12-13
19.12.99: 80-92 (*Caribbean Night Fever – Megamix*)

Hooray! Hooray! It's A Holi-Holiday is based on the melody of the nursery rhyme *Polly Wolly Doodle*, which was first performed by the Yale Glee Club in 1878, and published in a Harvard student songbook two years later. A young Shirley Temple sang the song in the 1935 musical, *The Littlest Rebel*.

The nursery rhyme was adapted by Frank Farian and Fred Jay, and recorded by Boney M., originally with the intention of including it and the B-side *Ribbons Of Blue* on the group's forthcoming fourth album, *OCEANS OF FANTASY*. However, of the two new songs, only *Ribbons of Blue* actually featured on the album when it was released.

'*Holiday* was something that made me laugh at first,' said Liz Mitchell. 'I couldn't believe that they really wanted us to do that song, but many people came up with the idea that we needed another song like *Brown Girl*, because so many people found a sweetness in it.'

Hooray! Hooray! It's A Holi-Holiday went to no.1 in Belgium, Denmark and the Netherlands, but it brought to an end Boney M.'s impressive run of seven chart toppers in a row in Germany, where it could only manage no.4. Elsewhere, the single achieved no.2 in Norway, no.3 in Austria and the UK, no.4 in Switzerland, no.5 in Ireland, no.6 in Spain, no.7 in Australia and New Zealand, no.11 in Sweden, no.12 in South Africa, no.14 in France and no.31 in Japan.

Hooray! Hooray! It's A Holi-Holiday was released a 7" picture disc single in the UK.

In 1999, *Hooray! Hooray! It's A Holi-Holiday* was remixed, as a single track and as a medley with *Brown Girl In The Ring*, *No Woman, No Cry* and *Calendar Song*, which was titled *Caribbean Night Fever*.

The remix charted at no.6 in Spain, equalling the peak achieved by the original release, but it was only a minor hit in Germany, New Zealand and Switzerland, and failed to chart in most other countries.

The Cheeky Girls released a cover of *Hooray! Hooray! It's A Holi-Holiday* in 2003, which they re-titled *Hooray Hooray (It's A Cheeky Holiday)* ~ it charted at no.3 in the UK, no.5 in Ireland, no.11 in Japan and no.40 in Germany.

14 ~ EL LUTE / GOTTA GO HOME

Germany: Hansa 100 804 (1979).

6.08.79: 7-7-**1**-**1**-**1**-**1**-**1**-**1**-**1**-**1**-2-2-2-3-4-5-7-7-12-10-11-9-19-20-47-51-40-61-64-58-62-x-69-72 (*El Lute*)

UK: Hansa/Atlantic K 11351 (1979).

11.08.79: 39-22-22-15-13-**12**-13-22-25-38-65 *(Gotta Go Home)*

Australia
1.10.79: peaked at no.**44**, charted for 20 weeks

Austria
15.09.79: **1**-**1**-3-7-12 (*El Lute*) (monthly/biweekly chart)

Belgium (Flanders)
4.08.79: 29-12-5-4-4-3-**2**-3-4-5-9-16

Canada
17.10.79: peaked at no.**11**, charted for 8 weeks *(Gotta Go Home)*

Denmark
10.08.79: 2-2-2-**1**-**1**-4-6-5-7-8-8-10-x-x-x-8-8-8-x-10-10 *(Gotta Go Home)*

EL LUTE

TEXT UND MUSIK: FRANK FARIAN / HANS BLUM / FRED JAY

Klavierausgabe mit Akk.- Bez.   Arr.: S. Klinkhammer

Auf HANSA 1oo8o4-1oo mit BONEY M.

ALLEINIGE AUSLIEFERUNG   **EDITION Intro**   Wittelsbacherstraße 18, 1000 Berlin 31

GOTTA GO HOME

Words and Music by FARIAN, HUTH, HUTH & JAY

Boney M

France
7.09.79: peaked at no.**5**, charted for 26 weeks (*Gotta Go Home*)

Ireland
12.08.79: 23-13-**11**-17-27-17-13-17-29 (*Gotta Go Home*)

Japan
10.10.79: peaked at no.**56**, charted for 11 weeks

Netherlands
11.08.79: 3-**2-2-2**-3-4-3-5-8-20-22-35-38

New Zealand
30.09.79: **42-42**-47-48-47-x-50 (*Gotta Go Home*)

Norway
11.08.79: 8-5-5-5-**4**-5-5-5-5-6-7-6-8-9-10

South Africa
20.10.79: peaked at no.**2**, charted for 16 weeks

Spain
21.01.80: peaked at no.**5**, charted for 10 weeks

Sweden
10.08.79: 12-11-**10**-11-13-12-18 (*El Lute*)

Switzerland
5.08.79: 10-4-**2-2-2-2-2-2**-4-4-5-6-9-11 (*El Lute*)

Following the success of *Rivers Of Babylon / Brown Girl In The Ring*, Boney M. released a string of double A-sided singles, starting with *El Lute / Gotta Go Home*, both lifted from the group's fourth studio album, *OCEANS OF FANTASY*.

Written by Frank Farian, Fred Jay and Hans Blum, *El Lute* was inspired by the true story of Eleuterio 'El Lute' Sánchez Rodríguez, who at one time was Spain's most wanted outlaw. At the time of the single's release, El Lute was in prison, convicted of a murder he claimed he didn't commit. Not long after *El Lute* became a hit, El Lute was pardoned and released from prison, and during a promotional visit to Spain Boney M. met him, and presented him with a gold record awarded for sales of *El Lute / Gotta Go Home*.

El Lute returned Boney M. to no.1 in Germany in a big way: it topped the chart for eight weeks, but it proved to be their last no.1. As the preferred A-side, *El Lute* also spent two months at no.1 in Austria, and charted at no.2 in Switzerland and no.10 in Sweden.

The second A-side, *Gotta Go Home*, was penned by Frank Farian and Fred Jay, based on Nighttrain's 1973 single, *Hallo Bimmelbahn* ~ this meant brothers Heinz and Jürgen Huth of Nighttrain also received a song-writing credit.

Gotta Go Home was the preferred A-side in several countries, achieving no.1 in Denmark, no.5 in France, no.11 in Canada and Ireland, no.12 in the UK and no.42 in New Zealand.

Where both *El Lute* and *Gotta Go Home* were listed alongside each other, the single charted at no.2 in Belgium, the Netherlands and South Africa, no.4 in Norway, no.5 in Spain, no.44 in Australia and no.56 in Japan.

Liz Mitchell re-wrote *El Lute* as *Mandela*, for Nelson Mandela, who was still in prison at the time, and recorded it for her debut solo album, *NO ONE WILL FORCE YOU*, released in 1988. *Mandela* was issued as single in a small number of countries, including the Netherlands and Spain, but it wasn't a hit.

Duck Sauce, *aka* DJs/record producers Armand Van Helden and A-Trak, sampled *Gotta Go Home* for their 2010 hit, *Barbra Streisand* ~ see later entry.

15 ~ I'M BORN AGAIN / BAHAMA MAMA

Germany: Hansa 101 101 (1979).

24.12.79: 49-41-9-**7**-19-13-10-12-16-20-22-31-32-36-40-50-51-55-66-62 (*I'm Born Again*)

UK: Hansa/Atlantic K 11410 (1979).

15.12.79: 50-38-38-36-**35**-45-62 (*I'm Born Again*)

Austria
15.01.80: 19-**9** (biweekly chart)

Belgium (Flanders)
22.12.79: 22-18-**16**-18-25-25-27

Denmark
1.02.80: **4**-7 (*I'm Born Again*)

France
7.03.80: peaked at no.**19**, charted for 6 weeks (*Bahama Mama*)

Ireland
16.12.79: 27-16-16-**12**-19-30-30 (*I'm Born Again*)

I'M BORN AGAIN
Words and Music by H. RULOF & F. JAY
Recorded by
BONEY M
on
ATLANTIC
Records
HANSA PRODUCTIONS LTD / ATV MUSIC LTD /
MUSIC SALES LTD · 78 Newman Street · London W1 · 60p

Japan
10.03.80: peaked at no.**63**, charted for 8 weeks (*Bahama Mama*)

Netherlands
22.12.79: 45-11-10-**7**-9-13-24-32-47

Sweden
11.01.80: **17** (*I'm Born Again*)

Switzerland
23.12.79: 15-15-10-**6-6**-8-10-14 (*I'm Born Again*)

Boney M. recorded *I'm Born Again* and *Bahama Mama* for their fourth studio album, *OCEANS OF FANTASY*, and together they were released as the album's second double A-sided single.

I'm Born Again was written by Fred Jay and Helmut Rulofs, and gave a nod towards Liz Mitchell's growing religious conviction (she had become a Born Again Christian). Although this song was the preferred A-side in most countries, it couldn't match the success of previous Boney M. singles, and there were worrying signs the hit formula was beginning to lose it mass appeal. *I'm Born Again* charted at no.4 in Denmark, no.6 in Switzerland, no.7 in Germany, no.12 in Ireland, no.17 in Sweden and a disappointing no.37 in the UK.

The second A-side, the more up-tempo *Bahama Mama*, was composed by Frank Farian and Fred Jay. On record, Bahama Mama was voiced by Linda Blake, who had previously appeared on an earlier Boney M. single as Ma Baker. *Bahama Mama* was the preferred A-side in fewer countries, achieving no.19 in France and no.63 in Japan.

Where both *I'm Born Again* and *Bahama Mama* were listed, the single charted at no.7 in the Netherlands, no.9 in Austria and no.16 in Belgium.

16 ~ I SEE A BOAT ON THE RIVER / MY FRIEND JACK

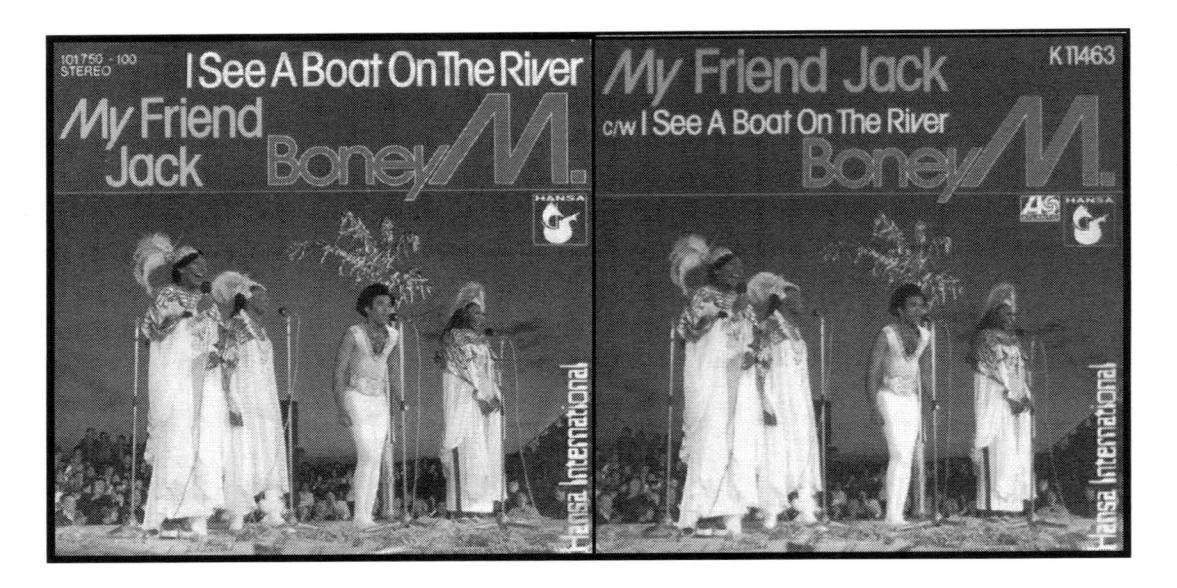

Germany: Hansa 101 750 (1980).

21.04.80: 37-7-7-**5**-7-8-7-6-12-14-13-16-13-21-24-33-30-44-45-45-56-55-64-52-72
(I See A Boat On The River)

UK: Atlantic K 11463 (1980).

26.04.80: 72-64-63-**57**-67 *(My Friend Jack)*

Australia
7.07.80: peaked at no.**81**, charted for 5 weeks *(My Friend Jack)*

Austria
15.05.80: 15-11-**3**-6-5-8-11 *(I See A Boat On The River)*   (biweekly chart)

Belgium (Flanders)
3.05.80: 22-13-12-10-**7-7**-10-12-19 *(I See A Boat On The River)*

Denmark
2.05.80: 5-3-3-3-**2**-7-7

France
30.05.80: peaked at no.**14**, charted for 7 weeks *(My Friend Jack)*

Japan
10.06.80: peaked at no.**70**, charted for 8 weeks (*My Friend Jack*)

Netherlands
10.05.80: 6-5-8-10-**4**-15-16-28-30 (*I See A Boat On The River*)

Norway
31.05.80: 10-x-8-**6**-9-7-8-9 (*My Friend Jack*)

South Africa
19.07.80: peaked at no.**4**, charted for 12 weeks (*I See A Boat On The River*)

Switzerland
11.05.80: 14-11-11-10-**9**-11-14 (*I See A Boat On The River*)

Zimbabwe
18.10.80: peaked at no.**7**, charted for 9 weeks (*I See A Boat On The River*)

Boney M. recorded *I See A Boat On The River* and *My Friend Jack* for their 1980 compilation album, *THE MAGIC OF BONEY M.*, and the two new tracks were released as a double A-sided single.

I See A Boat On The River was originally written by Frank Farian with Austrian singer Gilla and her fiancé, Helmut Rulofs. Fred Jay made some minor changes to the lyrics, so was also credited among the song's composers.

Of the two A-sides, *I See A Boat On The River* proved to be the most successful, and it achieved no.2 in Denmark, no.3 in Austria, no.4 in the Netherlands and South Africa, no.5 in Germany, no.7 in Belgium and Zimbabwe, and no.9 in Switzerland.

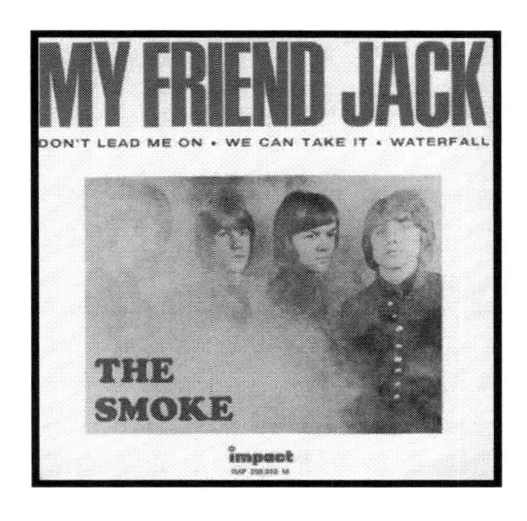

I SEE A BOAT ON THE RIVER

TEXT: FRED JAY / G. WINGER

MUSIK: HELMUT RULOFFS / FRANK FARIAN

Arr.: St. Klinkhammer

Klavierausgabe mit C-Melodie und Akk.-Bez.

Auf HANSA 1o175o mit BONEY M.

ALLEINIGE AUSLIEFERUNG — EDITION intro — Wittelsbacherstraße 18, 1000 Berlin 31

My Friend Jack was originally recorded by the English band The Smoke in 1967, for their debut album, *IT'S SMOKE TIME*. The song was credited to all four of the band's members: Geoff Gill, Zeke Lund, Mal Luker and Mick Rowley.

In the song, Jacks eats 'sugar lumps' ~ a reference to the psychedelic drug, LSD. EMI, The Smoke's record company, refused to accept the song in its original version, and even the toned down version that was finally released was banned by the BBC, which meant the single climbed to higher than no.45 in the UK. The single was more successful in Germany and Austria, where it achieved no.2 and no.6, respectively.

Boney M.'s cover of *My Friend Jack* charted at no.6 in Norway and no.14 in France, but stalled at a lowly no.57 in the UK, and was even less successful in Australia and Japan.

17 ~ CHILDREN OF PARADISE / GADDA-DA-VIDA

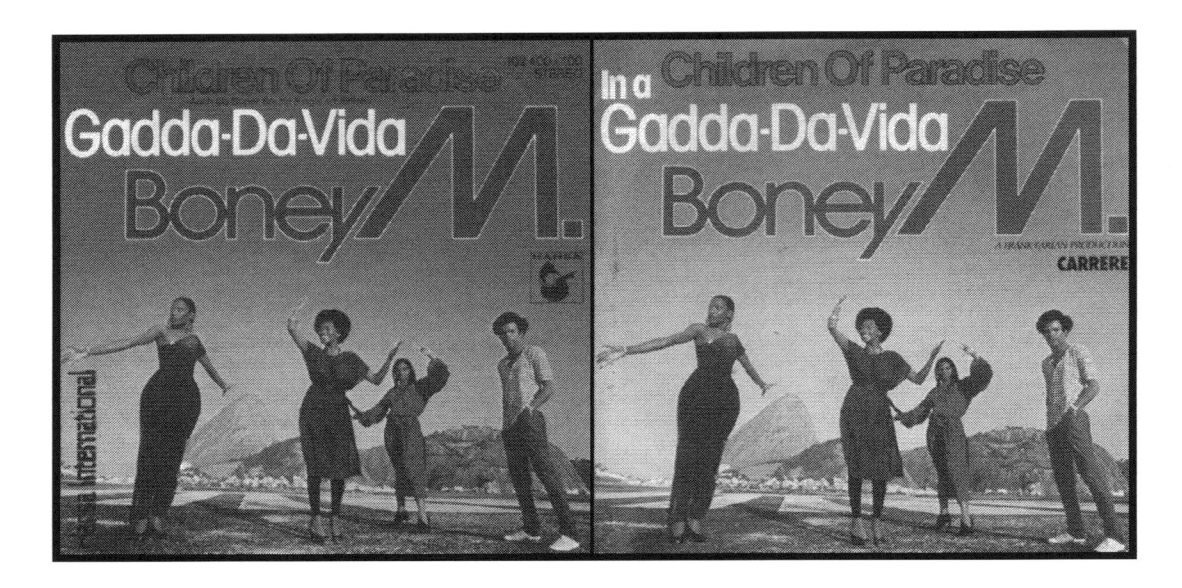

Germany: Hansa 102 400 (1980).

13.10.80: 68-47-12-**11**-15-17-16-16-28-25-28-27-34-23-57-54-59-71-66
(Children Of Paradise)

UK: Hansa/Atlantic K 11637 (1980).

14.02.81: 75-**66** (*Children Of Paradise*)

Austria
15.11.80: **12**-15-15-13-15 (*Gadda-Da-Vida*) (biweekly chart)

Belgium (Flanders)
25.10.80: 30-16-14-13-**11**-14-27 (*Children Of Paradise*)

Denmark
24.10.80: 6-4-4-**1**-2-2-4-2-10-10-10-9 (*Children Of Paradise*)

Netherlands
1.11.80: 43-**13**-20-20-27-29-46 (*Children Of Paradise*)

Children Of Paradise and *Gadda-Da-Vida* were originally recorded for Boney M.'s fifth studio album, which was scheduled to be released in November 1980. However, conflict between Frank Farian and the four members of Boney M. meant the album was delayed by a year, and when *BOONOONOONOOS* was finally released neither of these two songs featured on it.

Children Of Paradise was based on the song *Lili Twil* by Moroccan singer Younes Migri, and was composed by Frank Farian, Fred Jay and George Reyam. While it proved more popular than *Gadda-Da-Vida*, nevertheless *Children Of Paradise* failed to achieve Top 10 status anywhere. It went to no.1 in Denmark, and charted at no.11 in Belgium and Germany, no.13 in the Netherlands, and a lowly no.66 in the UK.

Gadda-Da-Vida – as *In-A-Gadda-Da-Vida* – was written by Doug Ingle, who recorded it with his band Iron Butterfly in 1968 for the album with the same title. As a single, Iron Butterfly took *In-A-Gadda-Da-Vida* to no.7 in the Netherlands, but it wasn't a hit in most countries.

Incredibly, and controversially once the truth emerged, Boney M's cover of *Gadda-Da-Vida*, as it was titled on all but the French single, wasn't recorded by any of the recognised members of Boney M.

The male vocals, as was the norm, were performed by Frank Farian, but the female vocals were recorded by a trio of session singers known as La Mama: Cathy Bartney, Madeleine Davis and Patricia Shockley. Just once, Boney M. did promote the song on TV, lip-synching to a song none of them had played any part in recording.

Gadda-Da-Vida charted at no.12 in Austria, but in most countries it was passed over, and *Children Of Paradise* preferred.

18 ~ FELICIDAD (MARGHERITA)

Germany: Hansa 102 681 (1980).
  B-side: *Strange*.

22.12.80: 69-49-7-11-8-7-8-8-9-7-14-8-**6-6**-15-17-24-31-34-46-49-45-47-48-71-66-69

UK: not released.

Austria
1.02.81: 11-7-**6**-14-13-15 (biweekly chart)

Denmark
16.01.81: 4-2-**1**-3-3-5

Switzerland
11.01.81: 12-7-5-4-**3**-4-6-11

Margherita (Love In The Sun), as *Felicidad (Margherita)* was originally titled, was written by Pino Massara and Rosella Conz, and was recorded in Italian by Massara in 1980 ~ as a single, *Margherita (Love In The Sun)* charted at no.5 in the Netherlands, no.10 in Belgium and no.59 in Germany.

An English version of the song, titled *Margarita (Mamma, Oh Mamma)*, was released in the UK but it wasn't a hit.

Frank Farian re-titled the song *Felicidad (Margherita)*, *Felicidad* being Spanish for 'Happiness'. Since tensions between him and the members of Boney M. were still running high, Frank repeated the trick he had pulled with *Gadda-Da-Vida*, and recorded the song as a non-album single with the same trio of session singers, La Mama.

This time, Boney M.'s record company Hansa stepped in, and refused to release the song under Boney M.'s name. Frank was forced to back down, and before the song was released vocals by Liz Mitchell and Marcia Barrett were overdubbed on the recording.

Felicidad (Margherita) charted at no.1 in Denmark, no.3 in Switzerland, and no.6 in Austria and Germany, but it wasn't a hit in most countries. In the UK, perhaps not surprisingly as Boney M's last five singles had peaked at no.3, no.12, no.35, no.57 and no.66, respectively, *Felicidad (Margherita)* was passed over as a single.

In 2008, to pay tribute to Barack Obama, newly elected President of the USA, Frank Farian re-wrote some of the lyrics, and re-recorded the song as *Felicidad America (Obama – Obama)* with singers Sherita O. and Yulee B.. Two versions of the song, English and Spanglish, were released in early 2009, but the single wasn't a hit anywhere.

19 ~ MALAIKA / CONSUELA BIAZ

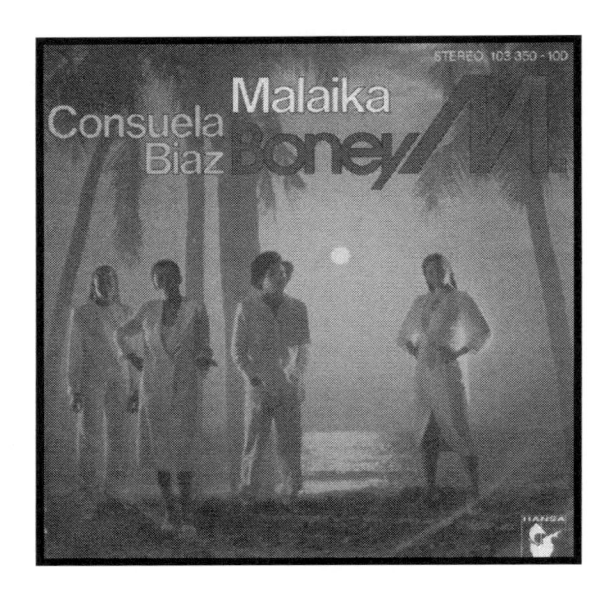

Germany: Hansa 103 350 (1981).

22.06.81: 31-15-15-**13-13**-15-15-16-17-26-43-40-45-55-59-73 (*Malaika*)

UK: not released.

Austria
15.07.81: 11-**7**-11-17 (*Consula Biaz*) (bi-weekly chart)

Belgium (Flanders)
8.08.81: 14-11-**8**-19-31-31-40 (*Malaika*)

Denmark
7.08.81: 9-9-8-6-**4**-15 (*Malaika*)

Netherlands
25.07.81: 22-22-16-**14**-22-33-38 (*Malaika*)

Spain
31.08.81: peaked at no.**6**, charted for 22 weeks (*Malaika*)

Switzerland
5.07.81: 14-7-**4**-5-6-6-7-12 (*Malaika*)

6/81
musik-informationen
mi
Die NEUE.
103 350-100
Malaika
Consuela Biaz
Boney M.
Der Superhit aus dem
MUSIK LADEN
Das neue Album »Boonoonoonoos«
kommt am 1. Sept. '81
HANSA
Hansa International
Im ARIOLA-Vertrieb

Boney M. recorded *Malaika* and *Consuela Biaz* for their much delayed fifth studio album, *BOONOONOONOOS*, and together they were released as the album's lead single.

Malaika was written, in Swahili, in 1945 by a Tanzanian musician, Adam Salim ~ the word translates as 'Angel', and refers to a beautiful girl. The song was first recorded in 1960 by Kenyan singer Fadhili Williams and his band, The Jambo Boys (also, later, known as The Malaika Boys). Williams also claimed to have written the song himself, but is only recognised as a composer of the song for royalty purposes.

Numerous other acts have recorded *Malaika* over the years, including the Hep Stars, a Swedish group whose members included ABBA's Benny Andersson.

Boney M. recorded *Malaika* with Liz Mitchell on lead vocals, with backing vocals by Liz, Marcia Barrett, Frank Farian and the session singers, La Mama. Not unusually, Frank released several different edits and mixes of the song, with the most popular featuring an outro with Frank himself singing 'Wimoweh, Wimoweh, Wimoweh …), borrowed from another song, *The Lion Sleeps Tonight*.

Malaika charted at no.4 in Switzerland, no.6 in Spain, no.8 in Belgium, no.13 in Germany and no.14 in the Netherlands.

Consuela Biaz, which proved the least popular of the two A-sides, was co-written by Frank Farian with Catharine Courage and Michael O'Hara. Once again, the lead vocalist was Liz Mitchell, with Liz, Marcia Barrett and Frank Farian – but not La Mama – on backing vocals.

Consuela Biaz rose to a respectable no.7 in Austria, but it wasn't a hit anywhere else.

Like *Felicidad (Margherita)* before it, *Malaika / Consuela Biaz* was passed over for single release in the UK.

20 ~ WE KILL THE WORLD (DON'T KILL THE WORLD) / BOONOONOONOOS

Germany: Hansa 103 666 (1981).

2.11.81: 43-20-**12**-14-19-17-18-26-16-27-23-23-26-26-39-47-51-65-64 (*We Kill The World*)

UK: Hansa/Atlantic K 11689 (1981).

21.11.81: 67-**39-39**-40-60 (*We Kill The World*)

Belgium (Flanders)
21.11.81: 32-22-**21**-29 (*We Kill The World*)

Denmark
13.11.81: 15-6-5-**3-3**-7-7-12

Netherlands
7.11.81: 45-50-26-28-32-29-36-20-**13**-14-24-42 (*We Kill The World*)

South Africa
16.01.82: peaked at no.**1** (for 3 weeks), charted for 22 weeks (*We Kill The World*)

Spain
22.02.82: peaked at no.**5**, charted for 13 weeks (*We Kill The World*)

Switzerland
8.11.81: 11-7-6-**3**-4-7-9-10-10-13   (*We Kill The World*)

Zimbabwe
8.05.82: peaked at no.15, charted for 8 weeks   (*Boonoonoonoos*)
22.05.82: peaked at no.**9**, charted for 9 weeks   (*We Kill The World*)

The second double A-sided single released from *BOONOONOONOOS* featured the title track and *We Kill The World (Don't Kill The World)*.

We Kill The World (Don't Kill The World) was written by Frank Farian with Giorgio & Gisela Sgarbi, and was a longer than usual track split into two parts, the up-tempo *We Kill The World* and the ballad *(Don't Kill The World)*.

For only the second time, after *Belfast*, *We Kill The World* featured Marcia Barrett on lead vocals on a Boney M. single. She was backed by Liz Mitchell and Frank Farian, with Bobby Farrell making a vocal contribution, albeit a spoken one, to a Boney M. recording for the first time.

The second, ballad half of the song featured a young boy, Brian Paul, on lead vocals. Brian was joined on backing vocals by his friend, Brian Sletten, together with Marcia, Liz, Frank and La Mama.

Several different edits of *We Kill The World (Don't Kill The World)* were released, and the single was most successful in South Africa, where it topped the chart for three weeks. Elsewhere, the single charted at no.3 in Denmark and Switzerland, no.5 in Spain, no.9 in Zimbabwe, no.12 in Germany, no.13 in the Netherlands, no.21 in Belgium and no.39 in the UK.

Caribbean slang for 'Happiness', *Boonoonoonoos* was written by Frank Farian, Fred Jay, Giorgio Sgarbi and Catharine Courage. The album version of the song was extended, leading into *That's Boonoonoonoos / Train To Skaville* and Van Morrison's *I Shall Sing*. Again, a numbers of edits were released, but the single was only listed on the chart in Zimbabwe, where *Boonoonoonoos* rose to no.15, before *We Kill The World (Don't Kill The World)* followed it into the chart and achieved no.9.

In Denmark, where both *We Kill The World (Don't Kill The World)* and *Boonoonoonoos* were listed, the single charted at no.3.

Plans to release *Jimmy* as the third single from *BOONOONOONOOS* were shelved.

21 ~ LITTLE DRUMMER BOY / 6 YEARS OF BONEY M. HITS

Germany: Hansa 103 777 (1981).

21.12.81: 34-36-**20**-38 (*Little Drummer Boy*)

UK: not released.

Belgium (Flanders)
2.01.82: 40-**14**-19-30-35 (*6 Years Of Boney M. Hits*)

Spain
14.06.82: peaked at no.**10**, charted for 7 weeks (*6 Years Of Boney M. Hits*)

The Little Drummer Boy was originally titled 'Carol Of The Drum', and was written by Katherine Kennicott Davis in 1941. The song was first recorded ten years later, by the Trapp Family Singers, but it didn't really become popular until 1958, when it was recorded by The Harry Simeone Chorale.
   Numerous other acts have recorded the song over the years, among them Joan Baez, David Bowie & Bing Crosby, Johnny Cash, Ray Charles, Destiny's Child, Neil Diamond, Jimmy Hendrix, Whitney Houston, The Jackson 5, Alicia Keys, Johnny Mathis, New Kids on the Block, The Supremes, The Temptations, Andy Williams and Stevie Wonder.

Boney M. recorded *Little Drummer Boy* for their *CHRISTMAS ALBUM*, which was rush-released in November 1981, mere weeks after *BOONOONOONOOS* appeared. Originally, the album was planned as a Liz Mitchell solo project, and Liz is the only member of Boney M. heard singing on *Little Drummer Boy*. However, she is joined by a young choirboy Michael Drexler, who sings the second verse. Following the relative failure of *BOONOONOONOOS*, Liz's *CHRISTMAS ALBUM* was released under Boney M.'s name instead of hers.

Little Drummer Boy achieved at no.20 in Germany, but it wasn't a hit anywhere else.

In 1981, a Beatles medley recorded by Dutch session musicians as Stars On 45 (Starsound, in some countries), was hugely popular, and this prompted Frank Farian to create a 13 minute Boney M. medley, which he titled *6 Years Of Boney M. Hits*. The songs featured on the full length version of the medley were *Let It All Be Music, Daddy Cool, Ma Baker, Belfast, Gotta Go Home, Love For Sale, Painter Man, Rasputin, Brown Girl In The Ring, Oceans Of Fantasy, Hooray! Hooray! It's A Holi-Holiday, Calendar Song, Dancing In The Streets, Bye, Bye Bluebird, Baby, Do You Wanna Bump, Rivers Of Babylon, Sunny* and *Nightflight To Venus*.

The short version (under five minutes), as released with *Little Drummer Boy* in Germany, omitted *Let It All Be Music, Love For Sale, Painter Man, Oceans Of Fantasy, Dancing In The Streets, Bye, Bye Bluebird* and *Nightflight To Venus*.

6 Years Of Boney M. Hits charted at no.10 in Spain and no.14 in Belgium.

22 ~ THE CARNIVAL IS OVER / GOING BACK WEST

Germany: Hansa 104 475 (1982).

26.07.82: **41**-48-44-43-49-51-55-74-73-56-65-60-69-61 (*Going Back West*)

UK: Atlantic A9973 (1982).

The Carnival Is Over / Going Back West wasn't a hit in the UK.

Denmark
3.09.82: 13-**12** (*The Carnival Is Over*)

Switzerland
18.07.82: 15-**11**-13-15 (*The Carnival Is Over*)

Zimbabwe
6.11.82: peaked at no.**1** (for 2 weeks), charted for 23 weeks (*Going Back West*)

The Carnival Is Over / Going Back West is the first single Boney M. released with their new member Reggie Tsiboe, who was brought in as a replacement for Bobby Farrell, after Frank Farian fired him from the group – a decision that wasn't popular with Boney M.s fans, as Marcia Barrett confirmed in her autobiography.

'Frank found out how popular Bobby was when he fired him in 1981,' she wrote, 'and tried to replace him: it just wasn't the same and the audience we'd built up was never happy about it.'

Based on a Russian folk song dating back to the 1880s, with English lyrics penned by Tom Springfield, *The Carnival Is Over* was recorded by The Seekers in 1965. It gave them a massive hit, topping the charts in the group's native Australia, Ireland and the UK, where the single sold more than a million copies. Elsewhere, the single charted at no.2 in South Africa, no.3 in Norway, no.5 in the Netherlands, no.8 in New Zealand and no.14 in Germany.

Frank Farian and Catharine Courage added an unnecessary, somewhat messy verse to Boney M.'s cover of *The Carnival Is Over*, to introduce new member Reggie Tsiboe, but the lead vocals on the recording were by Liz Mitchell.

The Carnival Is Over charted at no.11 in Switzerland and no.12 in Denmark, but it wasn't a hit anywhere else.

The second A-side, *Going Back West*, was written and originally recorded by Jimmy Cliff, for his 1971 album, *GOODBYE YESTERDAY*.

Boney M.'s cover of *Going Back West* featured new member Reggie Tsiboe on lead vocals, and the earliest version featured only La Mama on backing vocals ~ however, subsequent versions saw backing vocals by Liz Mitchell added, with Frank Farian also singing a few lines.

Going Back West hit no.1 in Zimbabwe and charted at no.41 in Germany but, overall, *The Carnival Is Over / Going Back West* was Boney M.'s least successful single since *Baby, Do You Wanna Bump*.

23 ~ JAMBO – HAKUNA MATATA (NO PROBLEMS)

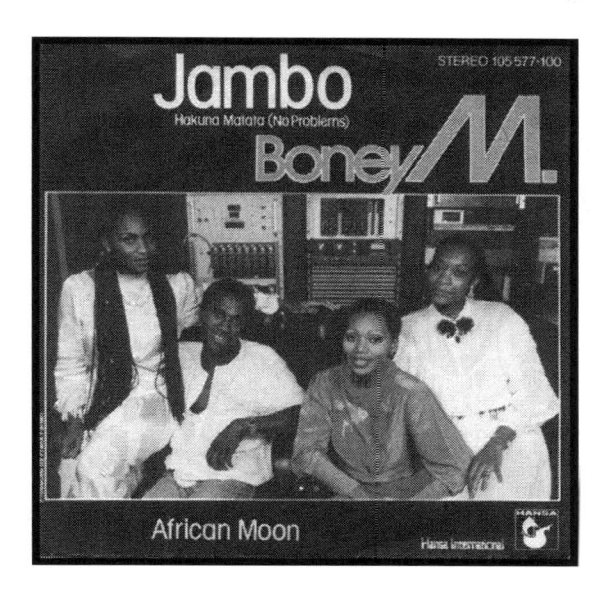

Germany: Hansa 105 577 (1983).
  B-side: *African Moon*.

19.09.83: 59-60-62-**48**-64

UK: Atlantic A9767 (1983).
  B-side: *African Moon*.

Jambo – Hakuna Matata (No Problems) wasn't a hit in the UK.

Switzerland
2.10.83: 15-14-**11**-15-x-15

Jambo – Hakuna Matata (No Problems) was originally titled *Jambo, Bwana*, meaning 'Hello, Sir' in Swahili. The song was written by Teddy Kalanda Harrison, and was originally recorded in 1981 by the Kenyan group, Them Mushrooms Band.
  Jambo, Bwana was hugely popular in Kenya, where it picked up a Platinum award, and was covered by numerous other African artists, including Mombasa Roots, Safari Sound Band and Adam Solomon.

Boney M.'s *Jambo – Hakuna Matata (No Problems)*, with English lyrics, featured Liz Mitchell on lead vocals, backed by Reggie Tsiboe, Frank Farian and La Mama. The single failed to arrest Boney M.'s declining sales, but it did achieve no.11 in Switzerland and no.48 in Germany.

Originally, *Jambo – Hakuna Matata (No Problems)* was planned as the lead single for a new Boney M. album, however, following poor sales it was dropped from the album that became *TEN THOUSAND LIGHTYEARS*.

Boney M. recorded *African Moon*, the B-side of *Jambo – Hakuna Matata (No Problems)*, for their *BOONOONOONOOS* album ~ the song was co-written by Liz Mitchell with Frank Farian, Catharine Courage and Helmut Rulofs.

24 ~ KALIMBA DE LUNA

Germany: Hansa 106 760 (1984).
  B-side: *10,000 Lightyears*.

10.09.84: 50-44-30-25-17-17-**16**-19-21-26-31-34-38-42-45-51-53-53-47-55-60-71-73

UK: Atlantic A 9619 (1984).
  B-side: *10,000 Lightyears*.

Kalimba De Luna wasn't a hit in the UK.

Austria
15.10.84: **11** (biweekly chart)

Belgium (Flanders)
6.10.84: 28-16-21-17-16-16-**15**-19-20-35

France
3.11.84: 26-34-26-27-15-14-9-7-9-7-**6**-8-12-13-18-24-33-28-34-46-43

Netherlands
1.11.80: 43-**13**-20-20-27-29-46

Spain
5.11.84: peaked at no.**5**, charted for 19 weeks

Kalimba De Luna was written by Tony Esposito, Guinluigi Di Franco, Mauro Malavasi, Remo Licastro and Giueseppe Amoroso, and was originally recorded by Esposito with Di Franco on vocals in 1984 ~ the single charted at no.6 in Italy and Switzerland, no.12 in Austria and no.25 in Germany.

Boney M.'s cover of *Kalimba De Luna* didn't actually feature any of the four members who made the group famous. It was recorded by new member Reggie Tsiboe, backed by Frank Farian and two session singers, Amy & Elaine Goff, and was originally planned as a Reggie Tsiboe solo single. Instead, Frank chose to release the song as a Boney M. single, and it was added to the group's current album, *TEN THOUSAND LIGHTYEARS*, plus the Boney M. compilation, *KALIMBA DE LUNA – 16 HAPPY SONGS*.

Kalimba De Luna was the first Boney M. single since *Baby, Do You Wanna Bump* that didn't feature the familiar 'Boney M.' logo, but that didn't stop it from giving the group their first Top 20 hit in Germany for three years. The single achieved no.5 in Spain, no.6 in France, no.11 in Austria, no.13 in the Netherlands, no.15 in Belgium and no.16 in Germany.

25 ~ HAPPY SONG

Germany: Hansa 106 909 (1984).
  B-side: *School's Out*.

10.12.84: 31-17-13-8-8-**7**-8-13-15-21-21-31-36-44-60-74-73

UK: Carrere CAR 354 (1984).
  B-side: *School's Out*.

Happy Song wasn't a hit in the UK.

Austria
15.02.85: 20-**15**-17-23-19 (biweekly chart)

Belgium (Flanders)
22.12.84: 34-32-30-**29**

Switzerland
3.02.85: 26-27-22-**21**-25-25-29

Happy Song was written by Abacap, and was originally recorded by the Italian disco group Baby's Gang, for their 1983, *CHALLENGER*.

Following Boney M.'s return to the charts with *Kalimba De Luna*, Frank Farian was keen to record a follow-up, which was credited to Boney M. and Bobby Farrell with The School-Rebels.

On *Happy Song*, Reggie Tsiboe shared lead vocals with a group of school children from Rhein-Main Air Base Elementary and Jr. High School, who were billed as The School-Rebels. Bobby Farrell contributed a rap, but once again Liz Mitchell and Marcia Barrett were absent, with session singers La Mama responsible for the female vocals.

Happy Song gave Boney M. what proved to be their final Top 10 single in Germany, where it peaked at no.7. Elsewhere, the single charted at no.15 in Austria, no.21 in Switzerland and no.29 in Belgium.

26 ~ MEGAMIX

France: Hansa 111 973 (1988).
 B-side: *Rasputin (Remix) (Radio Version)*.

18.03.89: 12-8-9-7-2-**1-1-1-1-1-1**-2-2-2-2-2-3-4-6-13-10-25-30-34

Belgium (Flanders)
6.05.89: 21-18-15-15-15-**11-11**-13-17

Megamix is a medley of hits Frank Farian remixed for the 1988 remix compilation, *GREATEST HITS OF ALL TIMES – REMIX '88*.

 The edited, single version of *Megamix* featured three Boney M. hits: *Rivers Of Babylon*, *Daddy Cool* and *Rasputin*. The extended, seven minute version released on 12" added a further two hits, *Ma Baker* and *Gotta Go Home*.

 Megamix was hugely popular in France, where it topped the chart for six weeks; it also charted at no.11 in Belgium but missed the chart in most countries.

27 ~ THE SUMMER MEGA MIX

Germany: Hansa 162 466 (1989).
  B-side: *Calendar Song*.

The Summer Mega Mix wasn't a hit in Germany.

UK: Ariola 112 497 (1989).
  B-side: *Calendar Song*.

2.09.89: **92**

Belgium (Flanders)
26.08.89: 29-**19**-33

France
12.08.89: 32-25-18-15-**11**-12-14-22-23-30-36

Norway
29.07.89: 8-5-4-**3**-6-5-5-7-7

The Summer Mega Mix, which featured on the 1989 remix compilation, *GREATEST HITS OF ALL TIMES – REMIX '89 – VOLUME II*, was a remixed medley of five Boney M hits: *Hooray! Hooray! It's A Holi-Holiday*, *Sunny*, *Kalimba De Luna*, *Ma Baker* and *Gotta Go Home*.

As with *Megamix*, an edited version of *The Summer Mega Mix* was released on 7", with the full seven and a half minute extended version issued as a 12" single.

The Summer Mega Mix achieved no.3 in Norway, no.11 in France and no.19 in Belgium, and spent a solitary week at no.92 in the UK.

28 ~ STORIES

Germany: Hansa 112 997 (1990).
 B-side: *Rumours (Instrumental)*.

Stories wasn't a hit in Germany.

UK: Ariola 112 997 (1990).
 B-side: *Rumours (Instrumental)*.

21.04.90: **94**

Switzerland
1.04.90: **26**

Stories was written by Bill Ador, Willy Albimoor and Jean Kluger, and was originally recorded in 1972 by the Belgian group, Chakachas.
 The British group Izit recorded an instrumental version of *Stories* in 1989, and it is this recording that Boney M.'s cover was loosely based on, with additional lyrics by Peter Bischof-Fallenstein.

As the 1980s drew to a close, Frank Farian had officially left Boney M. (even though he was never actually a member), and when Liz Mitchell failed to show for a concert she was hurriedly replaced by an American soul singer, Madeleine Davis, who joined Marcia Barrett, Maizie Williams and Bobby Farrell. The new line-up, keen to take Boney M. forward and record new music, got together with song-writer/producer Bobby Blue, to record *Everybody Wants To Dance Like Josephine Baker*, with Marcia on lead vocals.

Initial reaction to the new song was very positive, and it looked like the new Boney M. had a sizeable hit on their hands – until Frank Farian pulled the plug, and forced the last minute withdrawal of the single. It transpired Frank owned the copyright to the name 'Boney M.', and that legally only he was permitted to produce Boney M.

Everybody Wants To Dance Like Josephine Baker was subsequently released as a single in France, credited to 'Bobby Marcia Maizie Mataline *(sic)*', but it wasn't a hit and the whole episode left a sour taste in the mouth, with Marcia not shy of venting her anger at Frank in her autobiography: 'He was quite happy to have us tour to sell his greatest hits packages, which he continued to use our voices and images on, but he wasn't going to let anybody else produce (Boney M.) and make any money.'

Having effectively killed *Everybody Wants To Dance Like Josephine Baker*, Frank saw an opportunity to take advantage of the publicity generated, and produce a new 'official' Boney M. single.

Whereas *Everybody Wants To Dance Like Josephine Baker* had featured three of the four generally recognised members of Boney M., *Stories* featured only one: Liz Mitchell. She was joined by Reggie Tsiboe, plus two new female singers, Patty Onoyewerjo and Sharon Steven.

Stories charted at no.26 in Switzerland and spent one week at no.94 in the UK, but it flopped in most countries, and this lack of success finally spelled the end of Boney M. as a recording act.

29 ~ MEGA MIX

Germany: MCI 74321 12606 (1993).
  B-side: *Bang Bang Lulu*.

1.02.93: 81-x-**26**-27-**26**-31-36-38-44-45-87-85

UK: Arista 74321 12512 (1992).
  Double A-side: *Mary's Boy Child / Oh My Lord*.

5.12.92: 23-13-10-**7**-**7**-11-31-41-58-x-76-91-x-97

Austria
7.02.93: 16-**11**-15-23-19-22-16-21-24-29

Belgium (Flanders)
27.02.93: 50-47-47-**41**

Ireland
7.12.92: 10-5-**3**-4-20-9-8-16-27-24

Netherlands
30.01.93: 63-45-14-**12**-17-18-27-34

New Zealand
15.08.93: **49**

Yet another medley, *Mega Mix* featured five Boney M. hits: *Rivers Of Babylon*, *Sunny*, *Ma Baker*, *Daddy Cool* and *Rasputin*. The medley featured on the 1992 compilation, *GOLD – 20 SUPER HITS*, which was titled *THE GREATEST HITS* in the UK.

By now, of course, Boney M. no longer existed as the same group they once were, but the four original members were all still active musically, and touring with their own versions of Boney M. or as (Name) of Boney M. Liz Mitchell's line-up, which included Carol Grey, Patricia Foster and Curt Dee Daran, agreed to promote the single and album, and the result was Boney M.'s biggest single for many years.

Mega Mix charted at no.3 in Ireland, no.7 in the UK, no.11 in Austria, no.12 in the Netherlands, no.26 in Germany, no.41 in Belgium and no.49 in New Zealand.

BARBRA STREISAND

UK: All Around The World CDGLOBE 1472 (2010).
   Tracks: *Barbra Streisand (UK Radio Edit)/(Extended Mix)/(Afrojack Ducky Mix)/
   (Afrojack Meat Mix)*

23.10.10: **3-3**-7-9-18-25-26-38-45-50-45-38-44-52-73-86

Australia
10.10.10: 12-13-12-11-**9**-10-12-14-22-24-22-26-34-30-27-31-41-45-47

Austria
5.11.10: 18-9-2-2-**1**-2-2-2-2-2-4-7-14-24-20-17-25-31-33-47-50-51-50-66-61-74

Denmark
5.11.10: 18-11-13-5-**2-2**-4-6-4-5-6-10-12-11-9-16-17-35-31

Finland
23.10.10: 7-6-5-5-3-5-**1**-5-6-6-4-11-11-12-15-13-7-19-16-18-19

France
27.11.10: **3**-5-6-7-7-6-7-9-9-20-23-30-33-32-41-44-51-58-76-86-85-x-86-90-x-x-x-x-75

Netherlands
16.10.10: 25-2-2-**1-1-1**-3-6-14-19-14-9-9-22-28-25-34-39-51-69-71-55-63-84

New Zealand
4.10.10: 16-35-x-31-17-**11**-13-15-20-22-22-28-25-27-24-34

Norway
27.11.10: 18-15-19-17-10-7-**1**-4-5-7-7-13

Spain
31.10.10: 42-31-25-31-33-23-26-26-24-21-14-15-**6**-10-8-13-17-15-20-18-15-27-25-26-41-39-46-x-x-x-50

Sweden
5.11.10: 57-39-35-29-27-20-18-18-15-9-9-9-9-**8**-9-13-18-20-32-31-32-36-45-47-53-52

Switzerland
31.10.10: 57-24-4-3-2-**1**-**1**-2-2-2-**1**-**1**-**1**-2-4-7-10-11-12-16-19-22-26-31-37-39-43-54-51-x-x-x-x-72

Barbra Streisand is a hit by the duo Duck Sauce, comprising the American DJ, Armand Van Helden, and the Canadian DJ, A-Trak (aka Alain Macklovitch) ~ it extensively samples Boney M.'s 1979 hit, *Gotta Go Home*.

The single's cover was a re-modelled take on Barbra Streisand's 1980 album, *GUILTY*, on which she was pictured with Barry Gibb, who produced the album. Barbra's and Barry's faces were blanked out on *Barbra Streisand*, and duck bills added.

Barbra Streisand proved hugely popular, and hit no.1 in Austria, Belgium, Finland, the Netherlands, Norway and Switzerland, and charted at no.2 in Denmark, no.3 in France, Germany and the UK, no.6 in Spain, no.8 in Sweden, no.9 in Australia and no.11 in New Zealand.

30 ~ FELIZ NAVIDAD

Scandinavia: Ariola ARI 8250 (1982).
  B-side: *White Christmas*.

Feliz Navidad wasn't a hit in any Scandinavian countries.

Spain
12.12.10: 42-40-44
25.12.11: **32**

Feliz Navidad – meaning Merry Christmas in Spanish – was written and originally recorded in 1970 by José Feliciano. He took the song to no.1 in Sweden, no.4 in New Zealand, no.8 in Spain, no.21 in Germany and Switzerland, no.27 in Austria, no.30 in the Netherlands and no.44 in the USA.

Boney M. recorded *Feliz Navidad* for their 1981 album, *CHRISTMAS ALBUM*. The following year, it was released as a single in Scandinavia only, but it wasn't a hit anywhere.

Feliz Navidad found renewed popularity in 2010-11 in Spain where, thanks to digital downloads, the song charted at no.40 in 2010 and no.32 in 2011.

THE ALMOST TOP 40 SINGLES

Two Boney M. singles made the Top 50 in one or more countries, but failed to enter the Top 40 in any.

Somewhere In The World

Written by Wolfgang Keilhauer, Tammy Grohé, Sandy Davis, and featuring the London Philharmonic Orchestra, *Somewhere In The World* was the only single lifted from Boney M.'s 1984 album, *TEN THOUSAND LIGHTYEARS*. It featured lead vocals by Liz Mitchell, with Liz and Marcia Barrett on backing vocals. *Somewhere In The World* achieved no.49 in Germany, but it wasn't a hit anywhere else.

Young, Free And Single

Young, Free And Single was written by Frank Farian with Mary S. Applegate and Robert Reyen. Credited to Boney M. featuring Bobby Farrell, it was recorded for what would be the group's final studio album, *EYE DANCE*, released in 1985. Lead vocals were by Reggie Tsiboe, and Bobby Farrell's vocal contribution to the verses was heavily disguised by the use of a vocoder. The single charted at no.48 in Germany, but like *Somewhere In The World* it wasn't a hit anywhere else.

Note: no albums credited to Boney M., or any of the group's members, have peaked in the Top 50 in one or more countries, but failed to enter the Top 40 in any.

TOP 20 BONEY M. SINGLES

So, what is the most successful Boney M. single of all-time?

In this Top 40, each Boney M. has been scored according to the following points system.

Points are given according to the peak position reached on the albums chart in each of the countries featured in this book:

No.1:	100 points for the first week at no.1, plus 10 points for each additional week at no.1.
No.2:	90 points for the first week at no.2, plus 5 points for each additional week at no.2.
No.3:	85 points.
No.4-6:	80 points.
No.7-10:	75 points.
No.11-15:	70 points.
No.16-20:	65 points.
No.21-30:	60 points.
No.31-40:	50 points.
No.41-50:	40 points.
No.51-60:	30 points.
No.61-70:	20 points.
No.71-80:	10 points.
No.81-100:	5 points.

Total weeks charted in each country are added, to give the final points score.

Reissues and re-entries of a single are counted together.

Rank/Single/Points

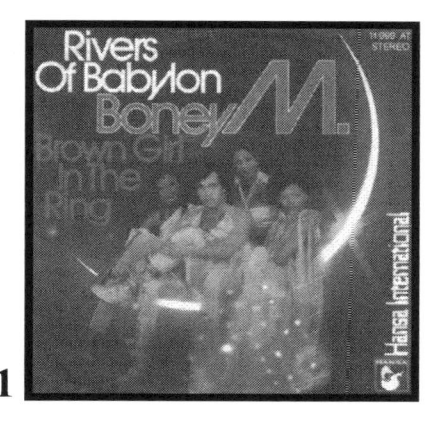

1 *Rivers Of Babylon / Brown Girl In The Ring –* 3394 points

2 *Daddy Cool –* 2368 points

3 *Ma Baker –* 2359 points

4 *Mary's Boy Child / Oh My Lord –* 1775 points

Rank/Single/Points

5 *Rasputin* – 1676 points

6 *Hooray! Hooray! It's A Holi-Holiday* – 1543 points
7 *El Lute / Gotta Go Home* – 1513 points
8 *Sunny* – 1450 points
9 *Belfast* – 1268 points
10 *I See A Boat On The River / My Friend Jack* – 924 points

11. *I'm Born Again / Bahama Mama* – 803 points
12. *We Kill The World (Don't Kill The World) / Boonoonoonoos* – 710 points
13. *Malaika / Consuela Biaz* – 604 points
14. *Kalimba De Luna* – 517 points
15. *Mega Mix* – 496 points
16. *Children Of Paradise / Gadda-Da-Vida* – 457 points
17. *Felicidad (Margherita)* – 398 points
18. *Painter Man* – 360 points
19. *The Carnival Is Over / Going Back West* – 333 points
20. *Happy Song* – 303 points

Not unexpectedly, *Rivers Of Babylon* and *Brown Girl In The Ring* comfortably emerge as Boney M.'s most successful single, with *Daddy Cool* pipping *Ma Baker* for the runner-up spot, and *Mary's Boy Child / Oh My Lord* taking fourth place ahead of *Rasputin*.

SINGLES TRIVIA

To date, there have been 29 Boney M. Top 40 hits, many of them double A-sides singles, plus one Top 40 hit by Bobby Farrell, in one or more of the countries featured in this book.

There follows a country-by-country look at the most successful Boney M. hits, starting with the group's home base, Germany.

Note: In the past, there was often one or more weeks over Christmas and New Year when no new chart was published in some countries. In such cases, the previous week's chart has been used to complete a chart run. Similarly, where a bi-weekly or monthly chart was in place, for chart runs these are counted at two and four weeks, respectively.

BONEY M. IN GERMANY

Boney M. achieved 24 hit singles in Germany, which spent 483 weeks on the chart.

No.1 Singles

1976	*Daddy Cool*
1976	*Sunny*
1977	*Ma Baker*
1977	*Belfast*
1978	*Rivers Of Babylon*
1978	*Rasputin*
1978	*Mary's Boy Child / Oh My Lord*
1979	*El Lute*

Most weeks at no.1

Boney M. spent 48 weeks at no.1 in Germany. The singles with the most weeks at no.1 are:

17 weeks	*Rivers Of Babylon*
12 weeks	*Daddy Cool*
8 weeks	*El Lute*
4 weeks	*Belfast*
3 weeks	*Ma Baker*

Singles with the most weeks

43 weeks	*Daddy Cool*
43 weeks	*Ma Baker*
37 weeks	*Rivers Of Babylon*
33 weeks	*El Lute*
27 weeks	*Belfast*
27 weeks	*Felicidad (Margherita)*
26 weeks	*Sunny*
25 weeks	*Hooray! Hooray! It's A Holi-Holiday*
25 weeks	*I See A Boat On The River*
23 weeks	*Kalimba De Luna*

BVMI (*Bundesverband Musikindustrie*) Sales Awards

Gold = 500,000, Platinum = 1 million

Platinum	*Rivers Of Babylon*
Gold	*Daddy Cool*
Gold	*Ma Baker*
Gold	*El Lute*

BONEY M. IN AUSTRALIA

Boney M. achieved 10 hit singles in Australia, which spent 206 weeks on the chart.

No.1 Singles

1978	*Rivers Of Babylon*
1978	*Rasputin*

Most weeks at No.1

6 weeks	*Rivers Of Babylon*
2 weeks	*Rasputin*

Singles with the most weeks

24 weeks	*Rivers Of Babylon*
23 weeks	*Daddy Cool*
23 weeks	*Rasputin*
22 weeks	*Ma Baker*

20 weeks   *El Lute / Gotta Go Home*
18 weeks   *Hooray! Hooray! It's A Holi-Holiday*

BONEY M. IN AUSTRIA

Boney M. achieved 17 hit singles in Austria, which spent 254 weeks on the chart.

No.1 Singles

1976   *Daddy Cool*
1976   *Sunny*
1977   *Ma Baker*
1978   *Rivers Of Babylon*
1978   *Rasputin*
1979   *El Lute*

Most weeks at No.1

16 weeks   *Daddy Cool*
16 weeks   *Rivers Of Babylon*
 8 weeks   *Ma Baker*
 8 weeks   *El Lute*

Singles with the most weeks

28 weeks   *Daddy Cool*
28 weeks   *Rivers Of Babylon*
24 weeks   *Ma Baker*
20 weeks   *Sunny*
20 weeks   *Belfast*
16 weeks   *Rasputin*
16 weeks   *Hooray! Hooray! It's A Holi-Holiday*
16 weeks   *El Lute*
14 weeks   *I See A Boat On The River*
12 weeks   *Mary's Boy Child / Oh My Lord*
12 weeks   *Felicidad (Margherita)*

BONEY M. IN BELGIUM (Flanders)

Boney M. achieved 21 hit singles in Belgium (Flanders), which spent 205 weeks on the chart.

No.1 Singles

1976	*Daddy Cool*
1976	*Sunny*
1977	*Ma Baker*
1977	*Belfast*
1978	*Rivers Of Babylon*
1978	*Rasputin / Painter Man*
1979	*Hooray! Hooray! It's A Holi-Holiday*

Most weeks at No.1

11 weeks	*Rivers Of Babylon*
6 weeks	*Ma Baker*
4 weeks	*Daddy Cool*
2 weeks	*Sunny*

Singles with the most weeks

25 weeks	*Ma Baker*
18 weeks	*Rivers Of Babylon*
14 weeks	*Belfast*
14 weeks	*Rasputin / Painter Man*
12 weeks	*Daddy Cool*
12 weeks	*Sunny*
12 weeks	*Hooray! Hooray! It's A Holi-Holiday*
12 weeks	*El Lute / Gotta Go Home*
10 weeks	*Mary's Boy Child / Oh My Lord*
10 weeks	*Kalimba De Luna*

BONEY M. IN CANADA

Boney M. achieved six hit singles in Canada, which spent 88 weeks on the chart.

The group's most successful single is *Rasputin*, which peaked at no.6.

Singles with the most weeks

32 weeks	*Rivers Of Babylon*
28 weeks	*Rasputin*
8 weeks	*Ma Baker*
8 weeks	*Gotta Go Home*

BONEY M. IN DENMARK

Since 1979, Boney M. achieved 11 hit singles in Denmark, which spent 84 weeks on the chart.

No.1 Singles

1979	*Mary's Boy Child / Oh My Lord*
1979	*Hooray! Hooray! It's A Holi-Holiday*
1979	*Gotta Go Home*
1980	*Children Of Paradise*
1981	*Felicidad (Margherita)*

Most weeks at No.1

3 weeks	*Mary's Boy Child / Oh My Lord*
2 weeks	*Hooray! Hooray! It's A Holi-Holiday*
2 weeks	*Gotta Go Home*

Note: Mary's Boy Child / Oh My Lord was no.1 on the first Danish singles chart, dated 5th January 1979; had the chart started earlier, it's likely the single would have topped the chart for more than three weeks.

Singles with the most weeks

17 weeks	*Gotta Go Home*
12 weeks	*Children Of Paradise*
10 weeks	*Hooray! Hooray! It's A Holi-Holiday*
9 weeks	*Mary's Boy Child / Oh My Lord*
8 weeks	*We Kill The World (Don't Kill The World) / Boonoonoonoos*
7 weeks	*I See A Boat On The River*
6 weeks	*Felicidad (Margherita)*
6 weeks	*Malaika*

BONEY M. IN FRANCE

Boney M. achieved 14 hit singles in France, which spent 316 weeks on the chart.

No.1 Singles

1976	*Daddy Cool*
1976	*Sunny*
1977	*Ma Baker*

1977   *Belfast*
1978   *Rivers Of Babylon*
1989   *Megamix*

Most weeks at No.1

6 weeks   *Megamix*
5 weeks   *Daddy Cool*
4 weeks   *Ma Baker*
4 weeks   *Rivers Of Babylon*
3 weeks   *Belfast*

Singles with the most weeks

50 weeks   *Ma Baker*
37 weeks   *Daddy Cool*
28 weeks   *Rasputin*
26 weeks   *Sunny*
26 weeks   *Gotta Go Home*
25 weeks   *Rivers Of Babylon*
24 weeks   *Megamix*
22 weeks   *Belfast*
22 weeks   *Hooray! Hooray! It's A Holi-Holiday*
21 weeks   *Kalimba De Luna*

BONEY M. IN IRELAND

Boney M. achieved 11 hit singles in Ireland, which spent 116 weeks on the chart.

No.1 Singles

1977   *Belfast*
1978   *Rivers Of Babylon*
1978   *Mary's Boy Child / Oh My Lord*

Most weeks at No.1

6 weeks   *Mary's Boy Child / Oh My Lord*
4 weeks   *Rivers Of Babylon*

Singles with the most weeks

34 weeks   *Rivers Of Babylon / Brown Girl In The Ring*

11 weeks	*Mary's Boy Child / Oh My Lord*
10 weeks	*Sunny*
10 weeks	*Mega Mix*
9 weeks	*Rasputin*
9 weeks	*Gotta Go Home*
8 weeks	*Belfast*
8 weeks	*Hooray! Hooray! It's A Holi-Holiday*
7 weeks	*I'm Born Again*
6 weeks	*Ma Baker*

BONEY M. IN JAPAN

Boney M. achieved nine hit singles in Japan, which spent 154 weeks on the chart.

The group's most successful single is *Rasputin*, which peaked at no.26.

Singles with the most weeks

40 weeks	*Sunny*
29 weeks	*Rasputin*
21 weeks	*Rivers Of Babylon*
16 weeks	*Hooray! Hooray! It's A Holi-Holiday*
14 weeks	*Ma Baker*

BONEY M. IN THE NETHERLANDS

Boney M. achieved 17 hit singles in the Netherlands, which spent 183 weeks on the chart.

No.1 Singles

1976	*Sunny*
1977	*Ma Baker*
1978	*Rivers Of Babylon*
1979	*Hooray! Hooray! It's A Holi-Holiday*

Most weeks at No.1

11 weeks	*Rivers Of Babylon*
6 weeks	*Ma Baker*
3 weeks	*Hooray! Hooray! It's A Holi-Holiday*

Singles with the most weeks

23 weeks	*Ma Baker*
23 weeks	*Rivers Of Babylon*
13 weeks	*Hooray! Hooray! It's A Holi-Holiday*
13 weeks	*El Lute / Gotta Go Home*
12 weeks	*Daddy Cool*
12 weeks	*We Kill The World (Don't Kill The World)*
11 weeks	*Belfast*
10 weeks	*Rasputin / Painter Man*

BONEY M. IN NEW ZEALAND

Boney M. achieved nine hit singles in New Zealand, which spent 145 weeks on the chart.

No.1 Singles

1978   *Rivers Of Babylon*

Rivers Of Babylon spent 14 weeks at no.1.

Singles with the most weeks

44 weeks	*Rivers Of Babylon*
28 weeks	*Ma Baker*
20 weeks	*Sunny*
16 weeks	*Rasputin*
15 weeks	*Hooray! Hooray! It's A Holi-Holiday*

BONEY M. IN NORWAY

Boney M. achieved 10 hit singles in Norway, which spent 166 weeks on the chart.

No.1 Singles

1976	*Daddy Cool*
1977	*Ma Baker*
1978	*Rivers Of Babylon*

Most weeks at No.1

10 weeks   *Daddy Cool*

9 weeks   *Ma Baker*
6 weeks   *Rivers Of Babylon*

Singles with the most weeks

36 weeks   *Daddy Cool*
29 weeks   *Rivers Of Babylon*
23 weeks   *Ma Baker*
19 weeks   *Sunny*
15 weeks   *El Lute / Gotta Go Home*
13 weeks   *Mary's Boy Child / Oh My Lord*
12 weeks   *Hooray! Hooray! It's A Holi-Holiday*
9 weeks   *The Summer Mega Mix*

BONEY M. IN SOUTH AFRICA

Boney M. achieved nine hit singles in South Africa, which spent 129 weeks on the chart.

No.1 Singles

1978   *Rivers Of Babylon*
1978   *Mary's Boy Child / Oh My Lord*
1982   *We Kill The World (Don't Kill The World)*

Most weeks at No.1

11 weeks   *Rivers Of Babylon*
3 weeks   *We Kill The World (Don't Kill The World)*
2 weeks   *Mary's Boy Child / Oh My Lord*

Singles with the most weeks

22 weeks   *We Kill The World (Don't Kill The World)*
21 weeks   *Rivers Of Babylon*
19 weeks   *Daddy Cool*
16 weeks   *El Lute / Gotta Go Home*
13 weeks   *Ma Baker*
12 weeks   *I See A Boat On The River*
10 weeks   *Hooray! Hooray! It's A Holi-Holiday*
10 weeks   *Mary's Boy Child / Oh My Lord*

BONEY M. IN SPAIN

Boney M. achieved 14 hit singles in Spain, which spent 230 weeks on the chart.

No.1 Singles

1976	*Daddy Cool*
1977	*Ma Baker*
1978	*Rivers Of Babylon*

Most weeks at No.1

7 weeks	*Daddy Cool*
5 weeks	*Rivers Of Babylon*

Singles with the most weeks

30 weeks	*Ma Baker*
27 weeks	*Rivers Of Babylon*
23 weeks	*Daddy Cool*
22 weeks	*Malaika*
20 weeks	*Hooray! Hooray! It's A Holi-Holiday*
19 weeks	*Kalimba De Luna*
18 weeks	*Rasputin*
16 weeks	*Sunny*
16 weeks	*Belfast*
13 weeks	*We Kill The World (Don't Kill The World)*

BONEY M. IN SWEDEN

Boney M. achieved eight hit singles in Sweden, which spent 95 weeks on the chart.

No.1 Singles

1976	*Daddy Cool*
1977	*Ma Baker*
1978	*Rivers Of Babylon*
1978	*Mary's Boy Child / Oh My Lord*

Most weeks at No.1

7 weeks	*Daddy Cool*
5 weeks	*Rivers Of Babylon*

3 weeks   *Ma Baker*

Singles with the most weeks

34 weeks	*Daddy Cool*
26 weeks	*Ma Baker*
14 weeks	*Rivers Of Babylon*
8 weeks	*Mary's Boy Child / Oh My Lord*
6 weeks	*Sunny*

BONEY M. IN SWITZERLAND

Boney M. achieved 16 hit singles in Switzerland, which spent 197 weeks on the chart.

No.1 Singles

1976	*Daddy Cool*
1977	*Ma Baker*
1977	*Belfast*
1978	*Rivers Of Babylon*
1978	*Mary's Boy Child / Oh My Lord*

Most weeks at No.1

14 weeks	*Daddy Cool*
14 weeks	*Rivers Of Babylon*
10 weeks	*Belfast*
5 weeks	*Mary's Boy Child / Oh My Lord*
3 weeks	*Ma Baker*

Singles with the most weeks

35 weeks	*Ma Baker*
26 weeks	*Daddy Cool*
21 weeks	*Rivers Of Babylon*
19 weeks	*Belfast*
13 weeks	*Sunny*
12 weeks	*Mary's Boy Child / Oh My Lord*
12 weeks	*Hooray! Hooray! It's A Holi-Holiday*
11 weeks	*Rasputin*

BONEY M. IN THE UNITED KINGDOM

Boney M. achieved 17 hits in the UK, which spent 191 weeks on the chart.

No.1 Singles

1978	*Rivers Of Babylon*
1978	*Mary's Boy Child / Oh My Lord*

Most weeks at No.1

5 weeks	*Rivers Of Babylon*
4 weeks	*Mary's Boy Child / Oh My Lord*

Singles with the most weeks

43 weeks	*Rivers Of Babylon / Brown Girl In The Ring*
28 weeks	*Mary's Boy Child / Oh My Lord*
16 weeks	*Ma Baker*
15 weeks	*Daddy Cool*
13 weeks	*Belfast*
12 weeks	*Mega Mix*
11 weeks	*Rasputin*
11 weeks	*Gotta Go Home*
10 weeks	*Sunny*
9 weeks	*Hooray! Hooray! It's A Holi-Holiday*

BRIT Certified/BPI (British Phonographic Industry) Awards

The BPI began certifying Silver, Gold & Platinum singles in 1973. From 1973 to 1988: Silver = 250,000, Gold = 500,000 & Platinum = 1 million. From 1989 onwards: Silver = 200,000, Gold = 400,000 & Platinum = 600,000. Awards are based on shipments, not sales; however, in July 2013 the BPI automated awards, based on actual sales since February 1994.

Platinum	*Rivers Of Babylon/Brown Girl In The Ring* (May 1978) = 1 million
Platinum	*Mary's Boy Child / Oh My Lord* (December 1978) = 1 million
Gold	*Rasputin* (November 1978) = 500,000
Gold	*Ma Baker* (December 1980) = 500,000
Silver	*Daddy Cool* (February 1977) = 250,000
Silver	*Painter Man* (April 1979) = 250,000
Silver	*Hooray! Hooray! It's A Holi-Holiday* (May 1979) = 250,000
Silver	*Gotta Go Home* (October 1979) = 250,000

BONEY M. IN THE UNITED STATES

Boney M. achieved four hit singles in the USA, which spent 30 weeks on the chart.

The group's most successful single is *Rivers Of Babylon*, which peaked at no.30.

Singles with the most weeks

17 weeks	*Rivers Of Babylon*
5 weeks	*Daddy Cool*
5 weeks	*Mary's Boy Child / Oh My Lord*

BONEY M. IN ZIMBABWE

Boney M. achieved 10 hit singles in Zimbabwe, which spent 138 weeks on the chart.

No.1 Singles

1977	*Ma Baker*
1978	*Rivers Of Babylon*
1982	*Going Back West*
1994	*Brown Girl In The Ring ('93 Remix)*

Most weeks at No.1

10 weeks	*Rivers Of Babylon*
4 weeks	*Ma Baker*
2 weeks	*Going Back West*

Singles with the most weeks

23 weeks	*Going Back West*
18 weeks	*Ma Baker*
17 weeks	*Daddy Cool*
13 weeks	*Rasputin*
12 weeks	*Mary's Boy Child / Oh My Lord*
10 weeks	*Rivers Of Babylon*
9 weeks	*I See A Boat On The River*
9 weeks	*We Kill The World (Don't Kill The World)*

All The Top 40 Albums

1 ~ TAKE THE HEAT OFF ME

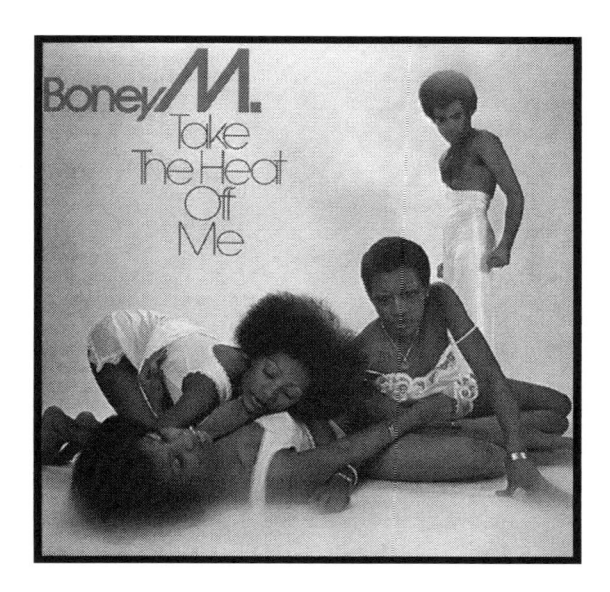

Daddy Cool/Take The Heat Off Me/Sunny/Baby, Do You Wanna Bump/No Woman No Cry/Fever/Got A Man On My Mind/Lovin' Or Leavin'

UK & USA: *Help Help* replaced *Baby, Do You Wanna Bump*.

Produced by Frank Farian.

Germany: Hansa 27 273 OT (1976).

15.10.76: 22-5-13 (monthly chart)-**2**-5-7-**2**-**2**-3-3-9-5-4-15-15-17-21-25-21-17-27-29-47-34-49 (biweekly chart)

UK: Atlantic K 50314 (1976).

23.04.77: 54-59-**40**-43-52

Australia
31.01.77: peaked at no.**26**, charted for 40 weeks

Austria
15.12.76: 10-11-**6**-11-19-17-x-25-22-x-21 (monthly chart)

France
11.02.77: peaked at no.**5**, charted for 34 weeks

Japan
25.11.77: peaked at no.**65**, charted for 15 weeks

Netherlands
15.01.77: 18-15-11-8-**5**-6-8-13-13-15-20

New Zealand
21.08.77: **34**-36-39

Norway
6.11.76: 19-16-13-8-9-7-5-6-7-7-5-6-5-5-6-4-4-5-4-4-4-4-3-3-**2**-3-3-3-3-3-3-3-5-9-6-8-9-7-12-6-9-9-14-14-12

Spain
21.03.77: peaked at no.**1** (for 2 weeks), charted for 28 weeks

Sweden
2.11.76: 18-8-2-2-2-**1-1-1**-2-2-2-2-3-4-7-10-11-12-13-19-19-23-35 (biweekly chart)

Switzerland
15.10.76: 21-24-**6**-9-12-18-21-22-17-25-18 (biweekly chart)

Zimbabwe
12.03.77: peaked at no.**6**.

> **BONEY M: 'Take The Heat Off Me'** (Atlantic K50314).
>
> Oddball band of three girls and a guy all born in the West Indies but based in Berlin — of all places. Their single 'Daddy Cool' which is included on this set has held the German Number One slot for many weeks. But then, that isn't too much of a feat. Germans tend to go for anything these days. They sing passable but very average glamourised reggae. ++

Boney M.'s debut album, like most of the group's future releases, was actually recorded by just two of the quartet, Liz Mitchell and Marcia Barrett, with producer Frank Farian contributing all the male vocals himself.

The album's title track was an English language cover of a 1974 Italian hit, *Nessuno Mai* by Marcella Bella. Frank produced a version of the song for the Austrian artist, Gilla, for her 1975 album, *WILLST DU MIT MIR SCHLAFEN GEHN?* (which translates as 'Do you want to sleep with me?'). The same album also featured Gilla's version of *Lovin' Or Leavin'*.

TAKE THE HEAT OFF ME was recorded at two studios in Germany, Europasound Studios in Frankfurt and Union Studios in Munich. Marcia sang lead vocals on the title track and *Lovin' Or Leavin'*, while Liz took the lead on four tracks: *Sunny*, *No Woman, No Cry*, *Fever* and *Got A Man On My Mind*.

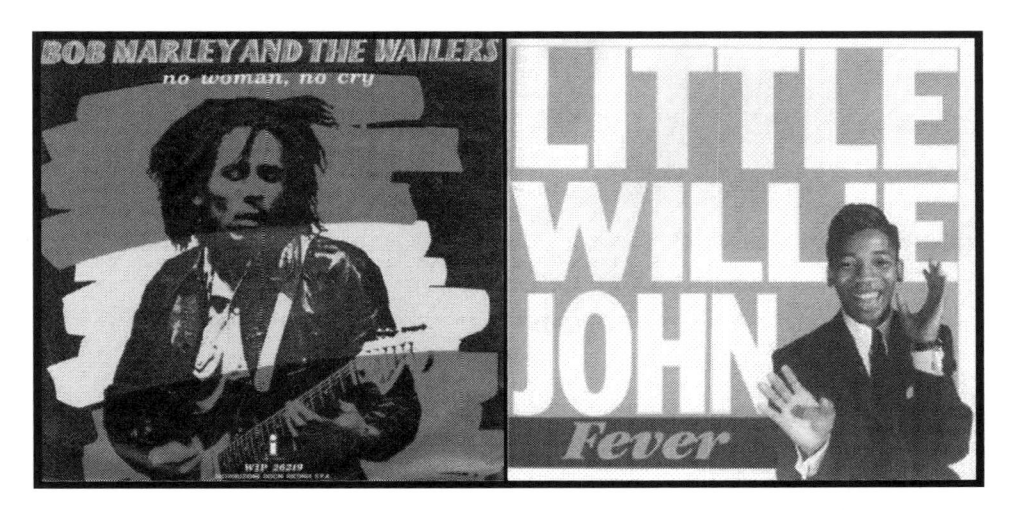

No Woman, No Cry, a cover of the popular Bob Marley & The Wailers hit from 1974, was the track Hansa wanted to release as the follow-up to *Baby, Do You Wanna Bump*, but Frank – wisely, as it turned out – insisted on *Daddy Cool* instead.

Fever and *Got A Man On My Mind* were also covers. *Fever* was originally recorded by Little Willie John in 1956, but is better known by Peggy Lee and, later, Elvis Presley, Madonna and Beyoncé. Frank adapted *Got A Man On My Mind* from *Am Samstagabend*, the B-side of his own German chart topper, *Rocky*. Interestingly, *Got A Man On My Mind* was issued as a single in Germany in 1977, credited to Liz Mitchell, but it wasn't a hit.

TAKE THE HEAT OFF ME went all the way to no.1 in Spain and Sweden, and achieved no.2 in Germany and Norway, no.5 in France and the Netherlands, no.6 in Austria, Switzerland and Zimbabwe, no.26 in Australia, no.34 in New Zealand and no.40 in the UK.

The album generated two hit singles, excluding *Baby, Do You Wanna Bump*, which was a hit before the group Boney M. was created:

- *Daddy Cool*
- *Sunny*

TAKE THE HEAT OFF ME was remastered in 2007, and released on CD with two bonus tracks:

- *New York City*
- *Perfect*

New York City was originally released as the B-side of *Sunny*, and *Perfect* was the B-side of Liz's solo single, *Got A Man On My Mind*.

2 ~ LOVE FOR SALE

Ma Baker/Love For Sale/Belfast/Have You Ever Seen The Rain/Gloria, Can You Waddle/ Plantation Boy/Motherless Child/Silent Lover/A Woman Can Change A Man/Still I'm Sad

North America: *Daddy Cool* replaced *Belfast*.

Produced by Frank Farian.

Germany: Hansa 28 888 OT (1977).

1.07.77: 6-2-**1**-**1**-**1**-3-4-11-7-14-19-30-34-37-41-29-31-42-36-31-27-27-21-31-31-31-21-37 (biweekly chart)-32-38-44-50-47-x-48

UK: Atlantic K 50385 (1977).

6.08.77: 42-16-18-**13**-17-24-35-54-x-x-56
27.05.78: 60

Australia
22.08.77: peaked at no.**27**, charted for 16 weeks

Austria
15.07.77: 3-**1**-**1**-4-13-14-18-14-x-23-x-x-16 (monthly chart)

Boney Mean

First 'Daddy Cool', then 'Sunny', now 'Ma Baker'...they're making it tough at the top.

Boney Magnificent

All four came from the West Indies - Marcia & Maizie going to London, Liz to Germany, & Bobby to Holland. Finally, they met in Munich...and the result to date is 9 gold discs.

Boney M

Their first album 'Take The Heat Off Me' (K50314) features their first two hit singles. Their new album 'Love For Sale' contains 10 great tracks. 'Ma Baker' gives you the taste...

LOVE FOR SALE
K 50385

Boney M.
Available on Atlantic/Hansa Records and Tapes

France
10.06.77: peaked at no.**1** (for 1 week), charted for 40 weeks

Netherlands
11.06.77: 15-6-5-3-3-**2-2**-3-3-5-7-8-12-14-19
3.12.77: 20

New Zealand
23.10.77: **22**-29-31-28-**22**-24-24-31

Norway
4.06.77: 8-3-**2-2-2-2-2-2-2-2-2-2-2-2-2-2-2-2-2**-3-3-5-5-11-12-13-x-x-x-16-16-16-15

Spain
26.09.77: peaked at no.**1** (for 7 weeks), charted for 42 weeks

Sweden
3.06.77: 13-**1-1-1-1-1**-2-2-3-4-6-10-21-47 (biweekly chart)

Switzerland
1.07.77: 4-**1-1-1**-3-3-3-6-5-4-8-x-12-18-12-5-20-16-23-11-13-10-7-6-5-24 (biweekly chart)

Zimbabwe
15.10.77: peaked at no.**4**.

The sleeve of Boney M.'s debut album was quite raunchy, but the sleeve of their second went much further, and featured lots of naked flesh and chains, but not much else.

'It was so much more porno-looking than *TAKE THE HEAT OFF ME*,' wrote Marcia Barrett in her autobiography, 'this time Frank (Farian) has come in with a bag of chains, handed them out and we literally couldn't believe it! We three girls didn't even know how we're supposed to wear them – if you can call it wearing them!'

'They wanted to photograph us all totally naked in chains with Bobby standing over us like it was bondage,' said Liz Mitchell. 'I wept, trust me. When they showed us the costumes, it was just heavy gold chains.'

Although they do appear naked on the sleeve, German photographer Didi Zill did allow Liz, Marcia and Maizie to keep their knickers on, but arranged them so they weren't visible, and so their breasts were covered.

'It's called *LOVE FOR SALE*,' said Maizie, 'so we posed in chains. No one today believes that we were wearing anything – I could show you a few photos that they threw out because the underwear was showing. They didn't want anything to show.'

'Why should I be ashamed of the sexy covers?' asked Marcia. 'They look good. We look naked, even though we're not.'

The group's North American record company, Atlantic Records, weren't impressed with the album's sleeve design, so chose instead to go with the photograph used on the back of the standard edition of the album. Atlantic didn't like the political nature of *Belfast*, either, so omitted it and added *Daddy Cool* in its place.

Like Boney M.'s debut album, LOVE FOR SALE featured a sprinkling of covers, including the title track, *Have You Ever Seen The Rain* and *Still I'm Sad*.

Love For Sale was composed by Cole Porter, Nelson Riddle, Buddy Gregman, Don Sickler, Geoffrey Mark Fidelman, Olavo Bianco and Comunicon, and was originally recorded by Ella Fitzgerald for her 1956 album, SINGS THE COLE PORTER SONG BOOK.

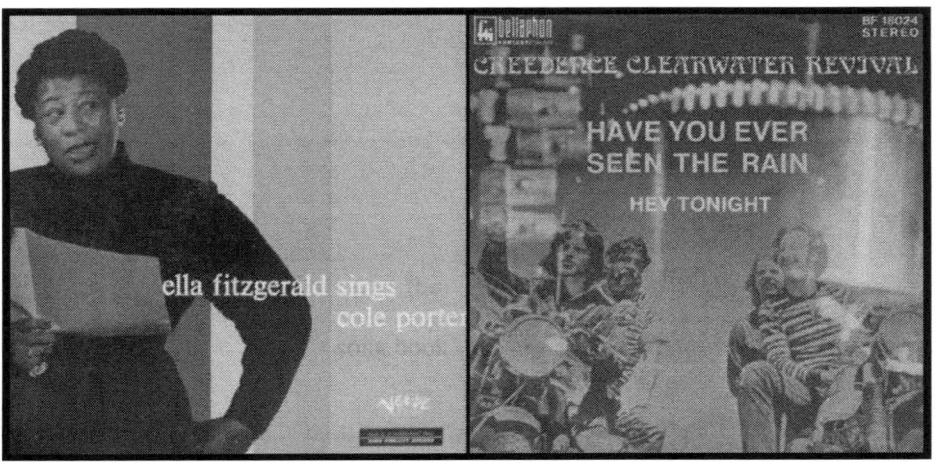

Have You Ever Seen The Rain was written by John Fogerty and Martin Bullard, and was originally recorded by Creedence Clearwater Revival in 1970, while *Still I'm Sad* originally featured on the 1965 album *OUR OWN SOUND* by The Yardbirds.

Motherless Child, originally titled *Sometimes I Feel Like A Motherless Child*, is a traditional song that dates back to the era of slavery in the USA.

Liz sang lead on six of the album's 10 tracks: *Love For Sale*, *Have You Ever Seen The Rain*, *Plantation Boy*, *Motherless Child*, *A Woman Can Change A Man* and *Still I'm Sad*. Marcia, once again, took the lead on two tracks, *Belfast* and *Silent Lover*, while producer Frank Farian sang the lead himself on *Gloria, Can You Waddle*.

The voice of Ma Baker on *Ma Baker* belonged to Linda Blake, while the spoken male voice on the same song was by Bill Swisher.

LOVE FOR SALE was hugely popular in continental Europe, where it topped the chart in Sweden for 10 weeks, in Austria for eight weeks, in Spain for seven weeks, and in Germany and Switzerland for six weeks. The album spent an incredible 17 weeks at no.2 in Norway, and charted at no.2 in the Netherlands, no.4 in Zimbabwe, no.13 in the UK, no.22 in New Zealand and no.27 in Australia. The album narrowly failed to break into the Billboard 200 in the USA, where it rose to no.6 on the 'bubbling under' chart.

LOVE FOR SALE generated three hit singles:

- *Ma Baker*
- *Belfast*
- *Still I'm Sad*

Still I'm Sad was released as the B-side of *Ma Baker* in most countries, but charted in its own right in Sweden.

LOVE FOR SALE was remastered in 2007, and released on CD with two bonus tracks:

- *Ma Baker/Somebody Scream (Sash! Radio Edit)*
- *Stories*

Stories was a curious choice as, as Boney M.'s final official single (excluding medleys and remixes), it wasn't released until 1990 – 13 years after the *LOVE FOR SALE* album.

3 ~ NIGHTFLIGHT TO VENUS

Nightflight To Venus/Rasputin/Painter Man/He Was A Steppenwolf/King Of The Road/ Rivers Of Babylon/Voodoonight/Brown Girl In The Ring/Never Change Lovers In The Middle Of The Night/Heart Of Gold

Produced by Frank Farian.

Germany: Hansa 26 026 OT (1978).

15.07.78: 2-**1**-**1** (biweekly chart)-**1**-**1**-**1**-**1**-**1**-**1**-**1**-2-3-4-3-4-4-4-4-3-4-3-4-5-5-6-4-7-9-13-22-23-25-25-31-42-33-41-41-42-26-33-38-42-46-43-47-x-35-40-42-48-47-47-x-47-x-43-46-38-46-42

UK: Atlantic K 50498 (1978).

29.07.78: 42-4-4-2-2-2-**1**-**1**-**1**-**1**-4-7-4-3-3-2-5-6-11-9-6-5-5-4-6-5-7-9-16-19-20-27-25-33-29-33-51-35-52-45-55-42-35-45-42-48-66-74-73
11.08.79: 55-75-65-x-71-x-x-33-44-59-53-73-74
15.12.79: 59-55-55-62-69-69

Australia
24.07.78: peaked at no.**7**, charted for 41 weeks

Austria
15.07.78: 2-**1**-2-3-3-3-9-15-21 (monthly chart)

148

Canada
24.02.79: 60-50-30-16-13-11-9-9-11-11-**7-7**-11-25-55-79-79

France
21.07.78: peaked at no.**2**, charted for 48 weeks

Boney M get the vote

BONEY M: 'Night Flight To Venus' (Atlantic K 50498)

"WELCOME shareholders to this, the third and biggest annual convention of the Boney M corporation.

The curtains roll back to reveal a glittering black cabinet bathed in dazzling laser light.

Computerised percussion begins to blast forth from hidden speakers, the hypnotic noise soon augmented by ethereal voices that float around the room. Dissenters, if indeed there were any, are soon converted, the rapt audiences responsing to the aural assault by clapping and tapping and shaking their heads. The strains of the song can be clearly heard at a distance.

"Your music floods the homeland
Boney M! Boney M!
Your fame has spread abroad,
Boney M! Boney M!
You're Europe's greatest show band
Boney M! Boney M!
Mightier than the sword!"

As the roars and thunderous applause greet the last rousing chorus the product itself appears 'Night Flight To Venus', a gatefold album featuring the photogenic leaders of the corporation: Bobby, Marcia, Maisie and Liz.

Credit, too, is rightly accorded other members of the multinational conglomerate, such as producer Frank Farian, a quartet of engineers and the essential endeavours of The Rhythm Machine.

It can be clearly seen, the shareholders note with satisfaction, that Boney M's million-selling hit 'Rivers Of Babylon' is included in the new package (with a different mix), as is the appealingly trilling 'Brown Girl In The Ring' (the B-side of the hit).

Also that they have recorded splendid versions of 'King Of The Road' and 'Heart Of Gold' in that special way that never fails to get Teutonic toes tapping. And that there are several tracks of undisputed Germandiscosoul brilliance, such as a phased and futuristic title track and a languorous 'Never Change Lovers In The Middle Of The Night'.

Yet the masterstroke, the seal of true genius, comes with 'Rasputin', a racy, bouncing and totally addictive ode celebrating the Mad Monk's talents as "Russia's greatest love machine".

The shareholders were spellbound, unable to intake of more breath. At last they believed the promise. 1978 was going to be Boney M's year! Forward with the corporation!

The gall, the polish, the perfection. Say it any language. Say it Boney M. You know they're the best. The greatest album since 'Love For Sale'!! (And yes, I do really mean it). ✦✦✦✦✦
JOHN SHEARLAW

Japan
25.08.78: peaked at no.**56**, charted for 14 weeks

Netherlands
8.07.78: **1-1-1-1-1**-5-6-5-6-7-10-8-7-6-5-10-8-16-19-28-22-21-22-26-30-29-40-26-28-40-47

New Zealand
20.08.78: 21-4-**3-3-3**-4-4-4-4-5-**3**-4-5-5-10-7-6-8-9-9-9-9-9-5-6-7-10-12-13-27-20-23-34-38-32-40
5.08.79: 40-44-33-38-37-29-41-47-35-39-48-38

Norway
1.07.78: 16-3-2-2-2-2-2-2-2-**1-1**-2-2-2-2-2-2-3-2-2-2-2-2-3-3-7-8-10-18-18-18-15

Spain
18.09.78: peaked at no.**1** (for 1 week), charted for 34 weeks

Sweden
14.07.78: 2-**1-1-1-1**-2-2-4-5-8-11-11-14-12-16-27-26 (biweekly chart)

Switzerland
15.07.78: 2-**1-1**-2-4-6-8-4-14-14-25-x-13 (biweekly chart)

Zimbabwe
2.09.78: peaked at no.**1** (2 wks) (as *RIVERS OF BABYLON*)

Boney M.'s third album proved to be even more successful than their second, and hit no.1 in numerous countries.

The album featured covers of two well-known songs, *Heart Of Gold* and *King Of The Road*. The former was written and originally recorded by Canadian singer-songwriter Neil Young in 1971, and he took the song to no.1 in Canada and the USA, no.4 in Norway, no.9 in the Netherlands, no.10 in New Zealand and the UK, and no.12 in Ireland.

Roger Miller co-wrote and originally recorded *King Of The Road* in 1964 ~ his version hit no.1 in Norway and the UK, and charted at no.4 in the USA, no.5 in Ireland and no.10 in Canada.

Marcia Barrett gave an insight into how songs were selected for Boney M. albums, saying, 'For our albums, he (Frank Farian) takes about thirty songs and we do demos for all of them. He has about eighty percent of the say of what ends up on the record.'

Liz Mitchell contributed lead vocals to four of the 10 tracks on *NIGHTFLIGHT TO VENUS*, namely *Painter Man*, *Rivers Of Babylon*, *Brown Girl In The Ring* and *Heart Of Gold*. Marcia sang lead on three tracks, the title track, *King Of The Road* and *Never Change Lovers In The Middle Of The Night*, while producer Frank Farian sang lead on two tracks, *Rasputin* and *Voodoonight*.

The robotic voice on *Nightflight To Venus* belonged to Bill Swisher, and he was also heard as the narrator on *Rasputin*.

Four versions of *NIGHTFLIGHT TO VENUS* were released, best identified by the duration of the title track and the title track plus *Rasputin*:

- 1st version: 7:09 minutes (13:37 minutes with *Rasputin*).
- 2nd version: 5:55 minutes (11:58 minutes with *Rasputin*).
- 3rd version: 4:58 minutes (10:48 minutes with *Rasputin*).
- 4th version: 4:46 minutes (10:36 minutes with *Rasputin*).

The 4th version is considered to be the final or finished version, and is the most common – it is the version that appeared an all CD pressings of the album.

NIGHTFLIGHT TO VENUS was hugely popular in Germany, where it topped the chart for 11 weeks, and went on to sell over a million copies. It also gave Boney M. their first no.1 album in the UK, and also went to no.1 in Austria, the Netherlands, Norway, Spain, Sweden, Switzerland and Zimbabwe (the album was re-titled *RIVERS OF BABYLON* in southern Africa).

Elsewhere, *NIGHTFLIGHT TO VENUS* charted at no.2 in France, no.3 in New Zealand, no.7 in Australia and Canada, and no.56 in Japan. In the USA, the album became Boney M's first Billboard 200 entry, but it only climbed as high as no.134.

Four of the ten tracks on *NIGHTFLIGHT TO VENUS* became hit singles:

- *Rivers Of Babylon*
- *Brown Girl In The Ring*
- *Rasputin*
- *Painter Man*

Brown Girl In The Ring was released as the B-side of *Rivers Of Babylon*, but became popular in its own right as *Rivers Of Babylon* faded, leading to it being listed alongside *Rivers Of Babylon* on many charts. In most countries, *Painter Man* was released as the B-side of *Rasputin*, but in Ireland and the UK it was released as the follow-up to *Rasputin* and became a Top 10 hit.

Voodoonight, backed with *Heart Of Gold*, was released as a single in Japan, while the same two tracks, but with *Heart Of Gold* as the A-side, were issued as a single in South Africa, but neither was a hit.

NIGHFLIGHT TO VENUS was remastered in 2007, and released on CD with two bonus tracks:

- *Mary's Boy Child / Oh My Lord*
- *Dancing In The Streets*

4 ~ BEST – SUPER SPECIAL ALBUM

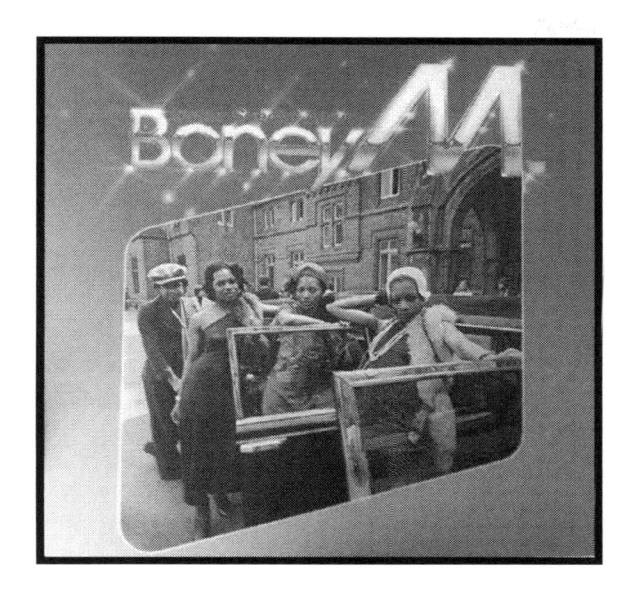

Rasputin/Voodoonight/Dancing In The Streets/Rivers Of Babylon/Ma Baker/Daddy Cool/ Sunny/Never Change Lovers In The Middle Of The Night/A Woman Can Change A Man/ Belfast/Love For Sale/Heart Of Gold

Japan: Atlantic P-10619A (1979).

10.05.79: peaked at no.**15**, charted for 21 weeks

This, the first Boney M. compilation album to achieve Top 40 status, was released exclusively in Japan. It comprised tracks from the group's first three albums and charted at no.15.

M 5078 C
Rocky
Mit großem Motor-Teil
Das teuflische Karussell INDIANAPOLIS
SANDOKAN
Der Ladykiller aus Indien
RIESENPOSTER
BMW-Phantom-Maschine
Trotz neuem Hit Krach bei Boney M.
Fliegt Bobby raus?
Das Buß-Konzert der
ROLLING STONES
Reportagen:
IAN HUNTER
BEE GEES
JANGO EDWARDS
RICHARD GERE
BLACK FÖÖSS
ROD + ALANA STEWART
Fotos, die keiner sehen sollte!
Die neuen WHO:
Überraschungs Konzert

5 ~ OCEANS OF FANTASY

Let It All Be Music/Gotta Go Home/Bye Bye Bluebird/Bahama Mama/Hold On I'm Coming/Two Of Us/Ribbons Of Blue/Oceans Of Fantasy/El Lute/No More Chain Gang/ I'm Born Again/No Time To Lose/Calendar Song

Argentina: *Hooray! Hooray! It's A Holi-Holiday* replaced *El Lute*.

Produced by Frank Farian.

Germany: Hansa 200 888 (1979).

1.10.1979: 8-5-**1-1**-2-2-3-3-4-4-10-12-12-11-13-15-15-18-22-12-21-29-26-23-16-23-20-27-35-52-34-42-x-53-x-51-x-34-35-60

UK: Atlantic K 50610 (1979).

29.09.79: **1**-2-3-5-7-13-18-34-33-48-47-54-45-50-50-37-50-68

Australia
29.10.79: peaked at no.**21**, charted for 16 weeks

Austria
15.10.79: **1-1**-4-(monthly chart)-12-12-x-20-x-13 (biweekly chart)

BRILLIANT BONEY M

Boney M.
Oceans Of Fantasy

Canada
19.01.80: 99-77-66-47-**44-44-44**-54-62-70-78

France
9.11.79: peaked at no.**1** (for 1 week), charted for 24 weeks

Japan
10.11.79: peaked at no.**51**, charted for 11 weeks

Netherlands
29.09.79: 23-**3**-4-6-14-18-21-28-39-42-48-43-30-49-29-27-37-26-41-35-42-39-49-41

New Zealand
11.11.79: 29-29-30-35-48-49
27.01.80: 49-22-23-21-**5**-16-28-43

Norway
22.09.79: 17-4-3-**1-1**-4-4-5-5-12-19-22-31-35-23-23-23-31-31

Spain
3.12.79: peaked at no.**1** (for 4 weeks), charted for 25 weeks

Sweden
5.10.79: 6-**5**-8-7-8-12-14-16-12-11-18-27-42 (biweekly chart)

Switzerland
1.10.79: 25-**1**-2-3-9 (biweekly chart)

Zimbabwe
15.03.80: peaked at no.**8**.

Boney M.'s fourth album *OCEANS OF FANTASY* featured 13 tracks, three more than their previous two albums.

The album was preceded by a non-album single, *Hooray! Hooray! It's A Holi-Holiday*, but despite the single being a sizeable hit it was left off the album. However, an edited version of the single's B-side, *Ribbons Of Blue*, was included on *OCEANS OF FANTASY*.

Four different pressings of *OCEANS OF FANTASY* were released, and on each one producer Frank Farian tinkered with several songs, either editing or remixing them ~ something he continued to do with the many Boney M. compilations that would be released over the years.

OCEANS OF FANTASY was the first Boney M. album to feature full vocal credits, which confirmed of the four group members, only Liz Mitchell and Marcia Barrett actually sang on the album, and that the male vocals were by producer Frank Farian.

Boney M.'s other two members, Maizie Williams and Bobby Farrell, did perform and sing during the group's live concerts.

Liz sang lead on six tracks: *Let It All Be Music, Two Of Us, Ribbons Of Blue, El Lute, I'm Born Again* and *Calendar Song*. She shared lead vocals on *Let It All Be Music* with Marcia, Frank and guest vocalist, Precious Wilson.

As well as *Let It All Be Music*, Marcia sang lead on *No Time To Lose*, while Frank shared lead vocals with Liz, Marcia and Precious Wilson on *Let It All Be Music*, with Liz on *El Lute*, and was lead vocalist on *Bye Bye Bluebird, Oceans Of Fantasy* and *No More Chain Gang*.

Precious Wilson came to Frank Farian's attention as the lead singer of Eruption, who enjoyed success with covers of Ann Peebles's *I Can't Stand The Rain* and Neil Sedaka's *One Way Ticket*.

Frank signed Eruption to Hansa International, and recruited the group as Boney M.'s support act and backing band, for their first European tour. Both Boney M. and Eruption appeared in the 1979 German film, *Disco Fever*, and later the same year Precious Wilson left Eruption, to pursue a solo career ~ she was replaced by Kim Davis.

The inclusion of *Hold On I'm Coming* on OCEANS OF FANTASY was strange, as Precious Wilson sang lead and backing vocals, with Frank joining her on backing vocals, but Liz and Marcia made no contribution to the recording at all.

Hold On I'm Coming, which was composed by Isaac Hayes and David Porter, and originally recorded by Sam & Dave in 1966, was issued as a single ~ credited to Precious Wilson, not Boney M.. It achieved no.45 in the Netherlands, but failed to chart in most countries.

Let It All Be Music, which also featured Precious Wilson on guest vocals, was released as a promo 7" and 12" single in Germany only, credited to Boney M. featuring Precious Wilson.

Bahama Mama featured Linda Blake as the voice of Bahama Mama, while Bill Swisher voiced the narrator on *El Lute*.

Two Of Us was composed by Paul McCartney, but was officially credited to 'Lennon-McCartney', in common with all Beatles recordings. The Beatles recorded the song in 1969, and it featured on their 1970 album, *LET IT BE*.

Although it couldn't match the sales of *NIGHTFLIGHT TO VENUS*, *OCEANS OF FANTASY* was very successful. It hit no.1 in Germany, Austria, France, Norway, Spain, Switzerland and the UK, and achieved no.3 in the Netherlands, no.5 in New Zealand and Sweden, no.8 in Zimbabwe, no.21 in Australia and no.44 in Canada.

Excluding *Hold On I'm Coming*, two hit singles, both double A-sides, were lifted from *OCEANS OF FANTASY*:

- *El Lute / Gotta Go Home*
- *I'm Born Again / Bahama Mama*

OCEANS OF FANTASY was remastered in 2007, and issued on CD with two bonus tracks:

- *I See A Boat On The River*
- *My Friend Jack*

Surprisingly, given it was released between *NIGHTFLIGHT TO VENUS* and *OCEANS OF FANTASY*, *Hooray! Hooray! It's A Holi-Holiday* wasn't included on the remastered CD of either album.

6 ~ THE MAGIC OF – 20 GOLDEN HITS

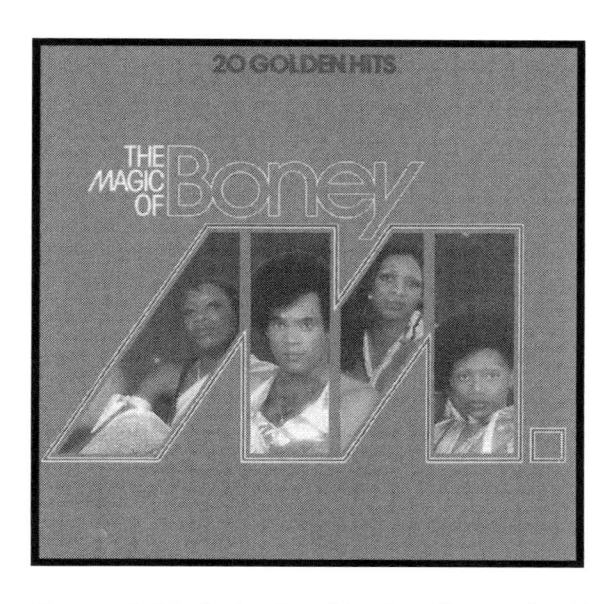

Rivers Of Babylon/Daddy Cool/Sunny/Belfast/El Lute/No Woman No Cry/Rasputin/ Painter Man/Ma Baker/Gotta Go Home/My Friend Jack/I See A Boat On The River/ Brown Girl In The Ring/Mary's Boy Child / Oh My Lord/Bahama Mama/I'm Born Again/Oceans Of Fantasy/Ribbons Of Blue/Still I'm Sad/Hooray! Hooray! It's A Holi-Holiday

Germany: Hansa 201 666 (1980), Hansa 30 943 5 (Club Edition, 1980).

5.05.1980: 3-**2**-3-4-**2**-**2**-3-7-5-8-11-16-18-21-25-23-20-28-44-42-33-41-48-54-64

UK: Atlantic BMTV1 (1980).

12.04.80: 18-6-10-3-2-**1**-**1**-2-7-10-13-15-21-22-23-28-36-41-48-44-38-56-75-69-65-67

Australia
26.05.80: peaked at no.**3**, charted for 22 weeks

Austria
1.06.80: 14-9-**5**-6-9-11-12-12-14 (biweekly chart)

Canada
4.11.78: ?-?-?-?-?-30-29-34-38
20.12.80: 45-45-45-45-45-23-**16**-17-23-?-?-?-38-40-42
7.11.81: ?-?-?-?-23-30-?

Netherlands
26.04.80: 30-**2-2-2-2-2**-3-**2**-12-8-23-16-20-34-22-14-47-42-48-36-39

New Zealand
15.06.80: 20-13-18-3-**2**-5-5-5-3-11-16-24-29-24-36-42-x-43

Norway
10.05.80: 24-x-37-29-15-**14**-18-15-26-24

Sweden
22.08.80: **30**-40 (biweekly chart)

Switzerland
15.05.80: 5-5-**4-4**-8-12-16-19-20 (biweekly chart)

Zimbabwe
1.11.80: peaked at no.**1** (11 wks)

Boney M.'s first internationally released compilation album featured three non-album singles, *Hooray! Hooray! It's A Holi-Holiday*, *I See A Boat On The River* and *My Friend Jack*, as well as most of the groups other hits and select album tracks.

The compilation featured the original album versions of *Daddy Cool* and *Painter Man*, plus an album edit of *Bahama Mama*, but all the other tracks on the album were necessarily edited, to ensure that 20 tracks could be included on the compilation.

In Germany, a Club Edition titled *GREATEST HITS OF* was issued with a different track listing:

Sunny/Daddy Cool/Belfast/Ma Baker/El Lute/Rasputin/I'm Born Again/Bahama Mama/

I See A Boat On The River/My Friend Jack/Gotta Go Home/Rivers Of Babylon/Mary's Boy Child / Oh My Lord/Brown Girl In The Ring/Ribbons Of Blue/Hooray! Hooray! It's A Holi-Holiday

THE MAGIC OF gave Boney M. their third chart topper from three releases in the UK, and spent an impressive 11 weeks at no.1 in Zimbabwe, but was less successful elsewhere, peaking at no.2 in Germany, the Netherlands and New Zealand, no.3 in Australia, no.4 in Switzerland, no.5 in Austria, no.14 in Norway, no.16 in Canada and no.30 in Sweden.

7 ~ BOONOONOONOOS

Boonoonoonoos/That's Boonoonoonoos/Train To Skaville/I Shall Sing/Silly Confusion/ Ride To Agadir/Jimmy/African Moon/We Kill The World (Don't Kill The World)/ Homeland Africa (Ship Ahoy)/Malaika/Consuela Biaz/Breakaway/Sad Movies/Goodbye My Friend

Produced by Frank Farian.

Germany: Hansa 203 888 (1981), Hansa 301 850-570 (Limited Edition 2LP, 1981).

16.11.1981: 59-**15**-18-21-27-31-31-24-21-24-34-28-39-43-49-45-63-x-52

UK: Atlantic K 50852 (1981).

BOONOONOONOOS wasn't a hit in the UK.

Austria
15.12.81: **14** (biweekly chart)

Netherlands
14.11.81: 47-37-43-40-x-x-40-**35**-37

Norway
14.11.81: 33-37-22-25-**21**-22-27-27-27-30-24-33-33-40

South Africa
26.12.81: peaked at no.**2**, charted for 24 weeks

Spain
14.12.81: peaked at no.**3**, charted for 21 weeks

Sweden
20.11.81: **31-31** (biweekly chart)

Switzerland
1.12.81: **5**-11-14-14-17 (biweekly chart)

Zimbabwe
10.04.82: peaked at no.**2**.

Although the recording of Boney M.'s fifth studio album began in the spring of 1980, the album *BOONOONOONOOS* wasn't actually released until September 1981.

Two of the newly recorded songs, *I See A Boat On The River* and *My Friend Jack*, were released as a double A-sided single, to promote the compilation, *THE MAGIC OF*. Later in 1980, a further two singles were issued: *Children Of Paradise / Gadda-Da-Vida* and *Felicidad (Margherita)*, backed with *Strange*.

At this time, thanks to an ongoing dispute over royalties, relations between Frank Farian and the four members of Boney M. were difficult, and one of the songs credited to Boney M. didn't feature any vocals by Liz Mitchell or Marcia Barrett: *Gadda-Da-Vida* was recorded by Frank Farian with three female session singers, La Mama.

Although she had no plans to leave Boney M., Marcia was keen to resurrect her solo career, and during 1980 she worked with songwriter Kelvin James and producer John Edmed, and came up with three new songs, *You*, *Breakaway* and *I'm Lonely*. She planned to release *You* as a single, with *Breakaway* on the B-side, before Frank Farian heard *Breakaway* and said he wanted to record it for Boney M.'s new album. Instead, *You* was released with *I'm Lonely* as the B-side.

Despite being agreeable to Marcia releasing a solo single, Frank Farian failed to use his influence with Hansa, to get behind *You* and promote it. In Marcia's words: 'It wasn't publicised or marketed or promoted properly, and I can't help but feel that wasn't by accident.'

New recording sessions took place in the spring of 1981, before Boney M. flew to Jamaica in May 1981 for a TV special. Whilst in the country, the quartet appeared live in concert with Rita Marley, took part in a photo shoot for their new album, and recorded one new song – *Silly Confusion* – at Bob Marley's Tuff Gong studios in Kingston.

Frank Farian originally envisaged BOONOONOONOOS as a double album, but it was released as a single album ~ however, the album was also issued as a limited edition double album, with the same track listing, but with some of the tracks featuring slightly longer versions than on the standard album.

The word 'boonoonoonoos' was invented by the Jamaican comedienne and folk poet, Louise 'Miss Lou' Bennett, and means anything or anyone beautiful and special.

Liz Mitchell sang lead on seven of the album's 13 tracks: *That's Boonoonoonoos / Train To Skaville / I Shall Sing, Jimmy, African Moon, Malaika, Consuela Biaz, Sad Movies* and *Goodbye My Friend*. Liz was also credited with co-writing *African Moon*.

Marcia Barrett was the lead vocalist on *We Kill The World (Don't Kill The World)*, and shared lead vocals with Frank Farian on *Breakaway*, with Frank taking the lead on *Ride To Agadir*.

For the first time, Bobby Farrell made a vocal contribution to a Boney M. album. He sang the rap on *Train To Skaville / I Shall Sing*, and voiced the spoken introduction to *We Kill The World (Don't Kill The World)*. The boy singing the 'Don't Kill The World' part of the latter is Brian Paul, and he and his friend Brian Sletten also sang backing vocals.

The session singers La Mama were credited with singing backing vocals on three tracks, *Silly Confusion, We Kill The World (Don't Kill The World)* and *Malaika*.

Shortly after BOONOONOONOOS was released, Frank Farian fired Bobby Farrell from Boney M., meaning the group were unable to promote the album as well as had been planned. Partly as a consequence, the album became the group's least successful to date, charting at no.2 in South Africa and Zimbabwe, no.3 in Spain, no.5 in Switzerland, no14 in Austria, no.15 in Germany, no.21 in Norway, no.31 in Sweden and no.35 in the Netherlands.

In the UK, where Boney M.'s last three albums had all gone to no.1, BOONOONOONOOS failed to chart, and as a result of ever less successful singles it was one of the few countries where the lead single *Malaika / Consuela Biaz* wasn't released. In most countries, two double A-sided singles were released from BOONOONOONOOS:

- *Malaika / Consuela Biaz*
- *We Kill The World (Don't Kill The World) / Boonoonoonoos*

BOONOONOONOOS was remastered and released on CD in 2007, with two bonus tracks:

- *Felicidad (Margherita) (Extended Original Version)*
- *Strange*

8 ~ CHRISTMAS ALBUM

Little Drummer Boy/White Christmas/Feliz Navidad/Jingle Bells/Winter Fairytale/Mary's Boy Child / Oh My Lord/Christmas Medley (Holy Night/Snow Falls Over The Ground/ Hear Ye The Message)/Petit Papa Noel/Zion's Daughter/When A Child Is Born/Darkness Is Falling/I'll Be Home For Christmas

Produced by Frank Farian.

Germany: Hansa 204 300 (1981).

4.01.1982: 18-**14**-42

UK: Atlantic K 50923 (1981).

MARY'S BOY CHILD – THE CHRISTMAS ALBUM wasn't a hit in the UK.

Australia
19.12.83: peaked at no.**53**, charted for 13 weeks

Canada
17.12.83: 94-93
11.11.89: 85-83-**80**-83-95-100

Netherlands
26.12.81: 17-11-**10**

New Zealand
13.12.87: **42-42**
24.12.95: 48

Spain
5.01.87: **37**

Recorded during the summer of 1981, *CHRISTMAS ALBUM* was originally going to be issued as Liz Mitchell's debut solo album. However, disappointing sales of *BOONOONOONOOS* prompted a re-think, and in an effort to boost Boney M.'s flagging popularity it was released as a Boney M. album instead ~ just three weeks after *BOONOONOONOOS* appeared.

The album included Boney M.'s 1978 festive hit, *Mary's Boy Child / Oh My Lord*, covers of popular Christmas songs and a couple of new songs. However, as with *BOONOONOONOOS*, the sacking of Bobby Farrell meant *CHRISTMAS ALBUM* didn't get the promotion or success it perhaps deserved.

Liz Mitchell, not surprisingly given it was supposed to be her solo album, sang lead vocals on most of the tracks. Marcia Barrett contributed backing vocals to just two of the new recordings, *Feliz Navidad* and *Jingle Bells*, while Frank Farian sang lead on *I'll Be Home For Christmas*. The choirboy heard singing the second verse of *Little Drummer Boy* is Michael Drexler.

The album produced one new hit single, *Little Drummer Boy*, which went Top 20 in Germany. *Feliz Navidad* was released as a single in Scandinavia, while Spain preferred *Jingle Bells*. The following year, *Zion's Daughter* was issued as a single in Germany, and *White Christmas* in Spain, but both failed to chart. The sleeve design for *Zion's Daughter* saw Reggie Tsiboe's photo replacing that of the departed Bobby Farrell.

CHRISTMAS ALBUM, which was titled *MARY'S BOY CHILD – THE CHRISTMAS ALBUM* in the UK, charted at no.10 in the Netherlands, no.14 in Germany and no.53 in Australia.

9 ~ THE VERY BEST OF

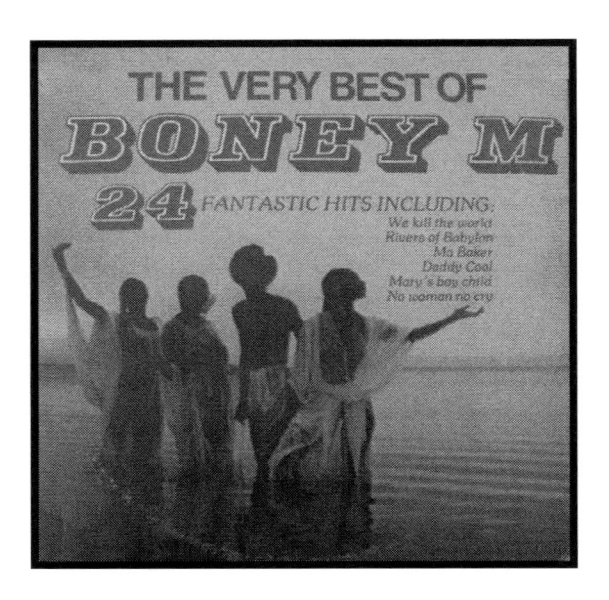

LP1: *We Kill The World (Don't Kill The World)/Rivers Of Babylon/Ma Baker/Daddy Cool/Mary's Boy Child / Oh My Lord/Brown Girl In The Ring/Belfast/Hooray! Hooray! It's A Holi-Holiday/El Lute/Sunny/Gloria, Can You Waddle/Painter Man*

LP2: *Rasputin/Take The Heat Off Me/Gotta Go Home/Ribbons Of Blue/A Woman Can Change A Man/Heart Of Gold/No Woman No Cry/Plantation Boy/Love For Sale/Fever/ Got A Man On My Mind/Children Of Paradise*

South Africa: Gallo DLPL 551/2 (1982).

7.08.82: peaked at no.**6**, charted for 25 weeks

This compilation, a double album, was released exclusively in South Africa, where it rose to no.6 and spent just one week shy of six months on the chart.

10 ~ CHRISTMAS WITH

O Tannenbaum (Oh Christmas Tree)/Joy To The World/Oh Come All Ye Faithful/The First Noel/Hark! The Herald Angels Sing/Little Drummer Boy/Somewhere In The World/Mother And Child Reunion/I'm Born Again/Children Of Paradise/Ribbons Of Blue/Mary's Boy Child / Oh My Lord/Hooray! Hooray! It's A Holi-Holiday/Auld Lang Syne

Germany: Hansa 206 733 (test pressing, 1984).

The release of CHRISTMAS WITH was cancelled in Germany.

UK: not released.

South Africa: Farian ML 4780 (1983).

3.12.83: peaked at no.**4**, charted for 8 weeks

Zimbabwe
11.12.83: peaked at no.**9**.

Following the success in some countries of Boney M.'s CHRISTMAS ALBUM, Frank Farian called Liz Mitchell and Reggie Tsiboe into the studio, to record songs for a new festive album ~ they were joined by two classically trained singers, twin sisters Amy & Elaine Goff.

Six new songs were recorded, before Frank had second thoughts. Then, following the success of the singles *Kalimba De Luna* and *Happy Song*, he decided to target the lucrative Christmas market with two new compilations, KALIMBA DE LUNA – 16 HAPPY SONGS and CHRISTMAS WITH BONEY M..

The original German test pressing of Boney M.'s second festive album brought together the six newly recorded songs with six songs with a seasonal or semi-religious theme to them:

O Tannenbaum (Oh Christmas Tree)/Oh Come All Ye Faithful/Joy To The World/Hark The Herald Angels Sing/The First Noel/Somewhere In The World/Mother And Child Reunion/I'm Born Again/Exodus (Noah's Ark 2001)/Ribbons Of Blue/Hooray! Hooray! It's A Holi-Holiday/Auld Lang Syne

Reggie was the lead vocalist on four of the six new songs: *Joy To The World, The First Noel, Mother And Child Reunion* and *Auld Lang Syne*. Liz took the lead on *Hark The Herald Angels Sing*, while Amy & Elaine Goff shared the lead vocals on *Oh Come All Ye Faithful*. The session group La Mama sang backing on *Mother And Child Reunion*, but Marcia Barrett didn't make a vocal contribution to any of the new songs.

CHRISTMAS WITH got no further than the test pressing stage in Germany, but Boney M.'s popularity was holding up in South Africa, so the album was released there, albeit with a slightly different track listing. Two songs, *Mary's Boy Child / Oh My Lord* and *Little Drummer Boy*, were added, and *Children Of Paradise* replaced *Exodus (Noah's Ark 2001)*.

The South Africa album is a rarity, and is sought after by Boney M. fans, not least because it included the original version of Paul Simon's 1972, hit, *Mother & Child Reunion*, which he took to no.3 in Norway, no.4 in the USA, no.5 in Canada and the UK, no.6 in the Netherlands, no.11 in Spain, no.15 in Ireland, no.23 in Germany and no.33 in New Zealand.

Frank Farian remixed and overdubbed additional vocals to *Mother And Child Reunion* in 1985, and released it as a charity single for Ethiopia, credited to Frank Farian Corporation featuring Reggie Tsiboe.

CHRISTMAS WITH rose to no.2 in Zimbabwe and no.4 in South Africa, but the rest of the world had to wait another two years, before the six new Boney M. songs were finally released on another festive compilation, *THE 20 GREATEST CHRISTMAS SONGS*.

11 ~ THE GOLD COLLECTION

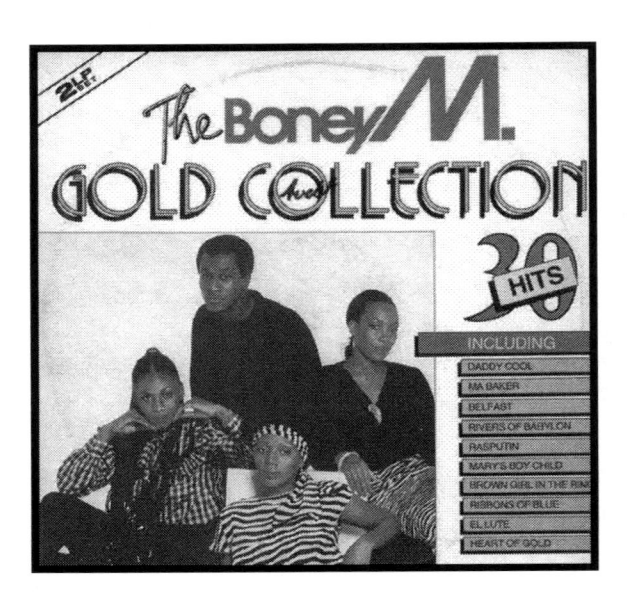

LP1: *Daddy Cool/Sunny/No Woman No Cry/Ma Baker/Have You Ever Seen The Rain/ Belfast/Plantation Boy/Rivers Of Babylon/Rasputin/Mary's Boy Child / Oh My Lord/ Hooray! Hooray! It's A Holi-Holiday/King Of The Road/Brown Girl In The Ring/ Nightflight To Venus*

LP2: *El Lute/I See A Boat On The River/Painter Man/Ribbons Of Blue/Got A Man On My Mind/I'm Born Again/Jimmy/Train To Skaville/I Shall Sing/We Kill The World (Don't Kill The World)/Boonoonoonoos/Gotta Go Home/Bahama Mama/My Friend Jack/No More Chain Gang/Heart Of Gold/Oceans Of Fantasy*

South Africa: Gallo DLPL 591/2 (1984).

2.06.84: peaked at no.**19**, charted for 1 week

THE GOLD COLLECTION was another double album released exclusively in South Africa, however, it couldn't match the success of *THE VERY BEST OF*, spending a solitary week on the chart at no.19.

12 ~ TEN THOUSAND LIGHTYEARS

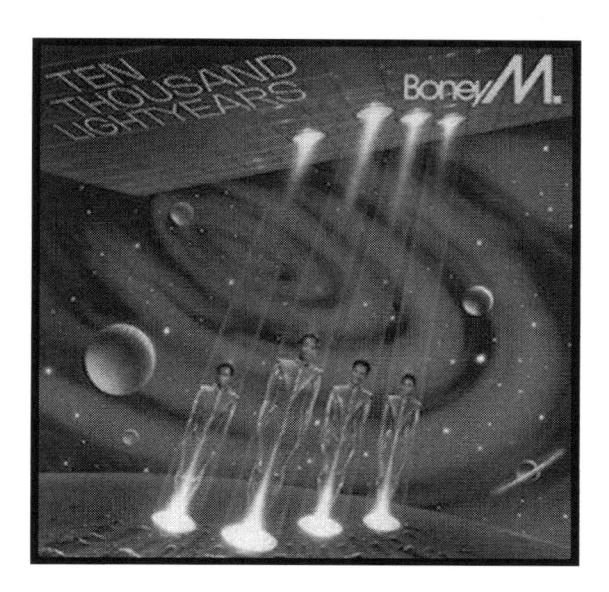

Exodus (Noah's Ark 2001)/Wild Planet/Future World/Where Did You Go/10,000 Lightyears/I Feel Good/Somewhere In The World/Bel Ami/Living Like A Moviestar/Dizzy/The Alibama/Jimmy/Barbarella Fortuneteller

Produced by Frank Farian.

Germany: Hansa 206 200 (1984), Hansa 41 094 4 (Club Edition, 1984).

18.06.1984: 64-x-49-x-65-x-61-x-27-**23**-25-27-34-35-48-46-43-52

UK: Hansa 206 200 (1984).

TEN THOUSAND LIGHTYEARS wasn't a hit in the UK.

Zimbabwe
2.09.84: peaked at no.**3**

Between 1976 and 1981, Boney M. averaged one new album a year ... then nothing.
 'In the three years between *BOONOONOONOOS* and the *CHRISTMAS ALBUM* in 1981 and *TEN THOUSAND LIGHTYEARS* in 1984 we didn't do any recordings,' Marcia Barrett confirmed in her autobiography. She stated: 'We were still out there performing live all over the world as a very popular touring act, but we had so little new material I felt as if time was standing still.'

Originally, the new album was planned as a continuation of the African themes explored on *BOONOONOONOOS*, with *Jambo – Hakuna Matata (No Problems)* slated as the lead single. However, *Jambo*'s lack of success meant it and the B-side *(I Need A) Babysitter* were both dropped, and the new album postponed for six months.

Boney M. – that is, Liz Mitchell, Marcia Barrett and Reggie Tsiboe, but not Maizie Williams – finally returned to the recording studio in the winter of 1983-84, with several of the new songs producer Frank Farian came up with having a sci-fi theme. The recognised members of Boney M. were joined on the album by La Mama and Amy & Elaine Goff.

Liz sang lead vocals on all the tracks on the album bar two, *Barbarella Fortuneteller* and a cover of Tommy Roe's 1969 hit, *Dizzy*, which topped the chart in Canada, the UK and the USA. Frank contributed the rap to *Dizzy*, while Amy & Elaine Goff were credited with backing vocals.

Reggie shared lead vocals with Liz on *Barbarella Fortuneteller*, and with Marcia on *Wild Planet*, which also featured Bill Swisher as the narrator. La Mama sang backing on four tracks, *Barbarella Fortuneteller*, *Future World*, *I Feel Good* and *The Alibama*. Mrs. Hanson and Children were credited with additional vocals on *Exodus (Noah's Ark 2001)*.

TEN THOUSAND LIGHTYEARS featured a new recording of *Jimmy*, a song which had originally appeared on *BOONOONOONOOS*. The song was re-recorded after Atlantic Records in the UK expressed as interest in releasing a more up-tempo version of the song as the follow-up to *We Kill The World (Don't Kill The World)*. However, by the time the song was ready, Atlantic had lost interest and no single was issued.

In Germany, four months after its initial release, *Kalimba De Luna* was added to *TEN THOUSAND LIGHTYEARS*, as the opening track of Side 2. The album charted at no.3 in Zimbabwe and no.23 in Germany, where it was the first Boney M. album to peak outside the Top 20.

TEN THOUSAND LIGHTYEARS was remastered in 2007, and issued on CD with two bonus tracks:

- *The Carnival Is Over (Goodbye True Lover)*
- *(I Need A) Babysitter (New Mix)*

Boney M.'s eighth and final studio album, *EYE DANCE*, was released 17 months after *TEN THOUSAND LIGHTYEARS*.

With Bobby Farrell having re-joined, Boney M. were now officially a quintet, but … vocally, the main focus was now on the group's newest member, Reggie Tsiboe, which meant Boney M. no longer sounded like the Boney M. their fans had grown to love. Liz Mitchell did sing lead vocal on two tracks, *Got Cha Loco* and *Chica Da Silva*, but overall she and Marcia Barrett made little contribution to the album's sound. Even the album's cover was pretty anonymous, and didn't feature a photograph of the group.

Two singles were released from *EYE DANCE*, a cover of Stevie Wonder's 1968 hit, *My Cherie Amour*, and *Young, Free And Single*, which featured vocoder vocals by Bobby Farrell. Both were minor hits in Germany, but the album itself bombed: it wasn't a hit, not even a minor hit, anywhere.

13 ~ 32 SUPERHITS – THE BEST OF 10 YEARS

Daddy Cool/Sunny/Ma Baker/Belfast/Rasputin/Painter Man/Children Of Paradise/Gotta Go Home/Dreadlock Holiday/Felicidad/Barbarella Fortuneteller/Gadda Da Vida/Got Cha Loco/Todos Buenos/No Woman No Cry/Brown Girl In The Rind/B.M. a GoGo (Medley) (New York City/Gloria, Can You Waddle/Baby Do You Wanna Bump/He Was A Steppenwolf/Bye Bye Bluebird/Nightflight To Venus)/Rivers Of Babylon/El Lute/The Calendar Song (January, February, March)/Bang Bang Lulu/Hooray! Hooray! It's A Holi-Holiday/Kalimba De Luna/My Cherie Amor/I Feel Good/Young, Free And Single/Happy Song

Germany: Hansa 207 500 (1986).

3.02.1986: 21-**3**-4-4-6-12-17-36-42-61

UK: Stylus SMR 621 (1986).

6.09.86: 47-**35**-38-45-80

Boney M. celebrated their 10th anniversary in 1986, and Frank Farian celebrated by creating a 46 minute medley of their hits, with added overdubs, which was billed as the 'Non Stop Digital Remix '86'.

32 SUPERHITS – THE BEST OF 10 YEARS saw Boney M. returning to the Top 10 in Germany, where the album rose to no.3. In the UK, where it achieved no.35, the album gave Boney M. their first hit album since *THE MAGIC OF* in 1980.

14 ~ THE VERY BEST OF

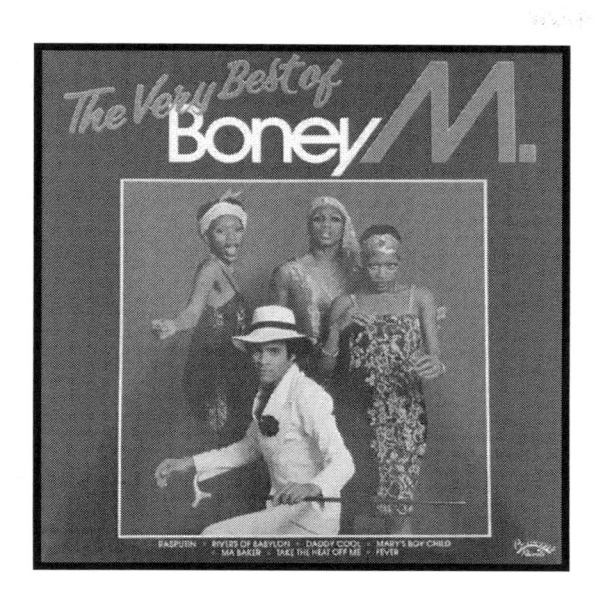

Rasputin/Rivers Of Babylon/Daddy Cool/Belfast/Mary's Boy Child / Oh My Lord/Hooray! Hooray! It's A Holi-Holiday/Love For Sale/Brown Girl In The Ring/Ma Baker/Sunny/No Woman No Cry/Nightflight To Venus/Take The Heat Off Me/Fever/Barbarella Fortune Teller/Oceans Of Fantasy

Australia: Concept Records CC 0052 (1986).

15.12.86: peaked at no.**30**, charted for 10 weeks

This 'Very Best Of' compilation was released exclusively in Australia and New Zealand ~ it peaked at no.30 in Australia, and spent 10 weeks on the chart.

15 ~ GREATEST HITS OF ALL TIMES – REMIX '88

Sunny/Daddy Cool/Rasputin/Ma Baker/Take The Heat Off Me/Hooray! Hooray! It's A Holi-Holiday/Rivers Of Babylon/No Woman No Cry/Brown Girl In The Ring/Gotta Go Home/Painter Man/Mary's Boy Child / Oh My Lord

Germany: Hansa 209 426 (1988).

UK: Ariola 209 476 (1988).

GREATEST HITS OF ALL TIMES – REMIX '88 wasn't a hit in Germany or the UK.

France
12.03.89: 14-14-**5-5**

Little more than two years after one Boney M. remix album, Frank Farian released another. This time, Liz Mitchell recorded new vocals for five of the remixes, and the group's new manager Simon Napier-Bell persuaded the four original members of Boney M. to reunite, albeit briefly, to promote the album.

The album was largely ignored in most countries, and owes its Top 40 status to its chart performance in France, where it spent two weeks at no.5.

Various remixes of *Rivers Of Babylon*, *Mary's Boy Child / Oh My Lord* and *Rasputin* were released as singles, but none enjoyed the kind of success Boney M. once did.

Megamix and *The Summer Mega Mix*, which Frank Farian created for *GREATEST HITS OF ALL TIMES – REMIX '89 – VOLUME II*, were more successful, but the album itself wasn't a hit anywhere.

16 ~ GOLD – 20 SUPER HITS

Rivers Of Babylon/Daddy Cool/Sunny/Brown Girl In The Ring/Rasputin/Ma Baker/ Hooray! Hooray! It's A Holi-Holiday/Painter Man/Belfast/No Woman No Cry/Mary's Boy Child / Oh My Lord/Gotta Go Home/Still I'm Sad/Nightflight To Venus/Felicidad/El Lute/Baby, Do You Wanna Bump/Kalimba De Luna/Happy Song/Mega Mix (Rivers Of Babylon/Sunny/Daddy Cool/Ma Baker/Rasputin)

Germany: MCI 74321 12577 2 (1993).

25.01.1993: 78-29-12-**5-5-5-5**-7-11-13-15-17-18-26-27-33-41-44-48-60-71-74-77

UK: not released.

Austria
7.02.93: 21-**6**-11-8-8-12-9-13-13-14-16-13-20-17-27-28

Canada
4.12.93: **77**

Netherlands
30.01.93: 66-11-**2-2-2-2**-3-5-7-9-9-15-19-14-10-12-23-24-26-40-47-48-47-45-45-47-48-
 48-43-48-52-54-56-76-98

New Zealand
11.07.93: 20-19-8-6-**2-2-2-2**-3-5-6-11-19-19-42-43-31-32-35-33-34-41-37-30-30-24-25-

25-29-10-**2**-12-25-42
18.02.96: 49

Norway
6.03.93: 12-8-**6-6-6-6**-15-14-19-20

Sweden
10.03.93: 22-**14**-24-27-39

Switzerland
14.02.93: 9-6-6-**5**-8-8-9-11-13-13-17-24-28-30

In 1992, an ABBA compilation titled *GOLD – GREATEST HITS* was released, and went on to become a multi-million seller.

Never one to pass up an opportunity, Frank Farian put together a new Boney M. compilation, and titled it *GOLD – 20 SUPER HITS*. Although the album sleeve of some editions claimed all the songs were 'Original Masters', this was stretching the truth, as Frank not only edited most of the hits chosen for inclusion, but also overdubbed them with synthesized percussion as well.

The compilation included a new *Mega Mix*, which enjoyed success as a single, as did a remix of *Brown Girl In The Ring* in some countries.

In most countries, *GOLD – 20 SUPER HITS* gave Boney M. their biggest hit album since the 1980 compilation, *THE MAGIC OF*. The album charted at no.2 in the Netherlands and New Zealand, no.5 in Germany and Switzerland, no.6 in Austria and Norway, and no.14 in Sweden.

GOLD – 20 SUPER HITS wasn't released in the UK, but another compilation album with a similar track listing was, titled simply *THE GREATEST HITS*.

17 ~ THE GREATEST HITS

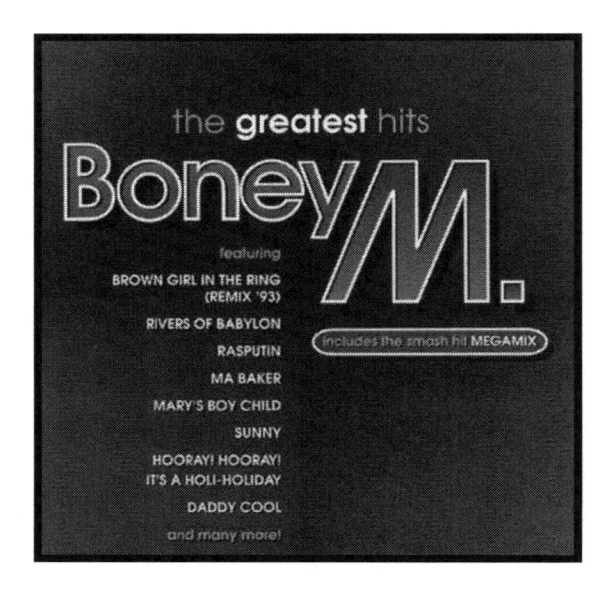

Rivers Of Babylon/Daddy Cool/Sunny/Brown Girl In The Ring ('93 Remix)/Rasputin/Ma Baker/Still I'm Sad/Hooray! Hooray! It's A Holi-Holiday/Painter Man/Belfast/No Woman No Cry/Mary's Boy Child / Oh My Lord/Gotta Go Home/Mega Mix (Rivers Of Babylon/ Sunny/Daddy Cool/Rasputin)

Germany: not released.

UK: Telstar STAR 621 (1993).

27.03.93: 23-20-**14**-17-24-25-36-25-37-70

In the UK and Ireland, a compilation titled *THE GREATEST HITS* was issued instead of *GOLD – 20 SUPER HITS*, although the track listing was similar and included the new *Mega Mix*, which went Top 10 in the UK.

THE GREATEST HITS rose to no.14 in the UK, and spent 10 weeks on the chart.

18 ~ MORE GOLD – 20 SUPER HITS VOL.II

Love For Sale/Bahama Mama/I See A Boat On The River/Children Of Paradise/Calendar Song/We Kill The World (Don't Kill The World)/Jimmy/I Shall Sing/Dreadlock Holiday/Oceans Of Fantasy/Ribbons Of Blue/Motherless Child/I'm Born Again/My Cherie Amor/Going Back West/Ma Baker ('93 Remix)/Time To Remember/Da La De La/Papa Chico/Lady Godiva

Germany: MCI 74321 16197 2 (1993).

MORE GOLD – 20 SUPER HITS VOL.II wasn't a hit in Germany.

UK: not released.

Austria
28.11.93: **38-38**-39-39-39

Netherlands
13.11.93: 89-88-**87**

New Zealand
20.02.94: **43**

South Africa
22.10.94: peaked at no.**5**, charted for 21 weeks

ABBA followed *GOLD – GREATEST HITS* with *MORE GOLD – MORE ABBA HITS* in 1993, so Frank Farian followed Boney M.'s *GOLD – 20 SUPER HITS* with *MORE GOLD – 20 SUPER HITS VOL.II*.

The new compilation, as well as some of Boney M.'s less successful singles, featured a remix of *Ma Baker* and four new songs, *Time To Remember*, *Da La De La*, *Papa Chico* and *Lady Godiva*. The new songs were all recorded in 1993, with Liz Mitchell singing lead on all four; she was joined on *Da La De La* by rapper Marlon B..

Ma Baker (Remix '93) and *Papa Chico* b/w *Time To Remember* were released as singles, the latter credited to Boney M. Feat. Liz Mitchell, but neither were hits.

MORE GOLD – 20 SUPER HITS VOL.II achieved at no.5 in South Africa, no.38 in Austria and no.43 in New Zealand, but failed to chart in most countries.

19 ~ BEST IN SPAIN

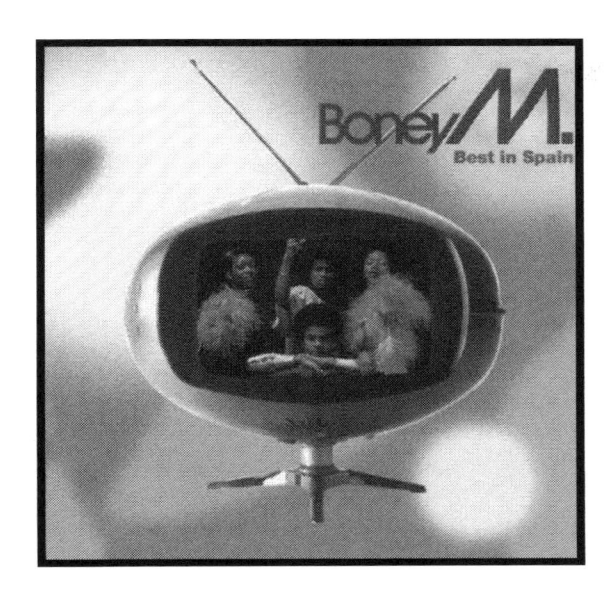

Daddy Cool/Rivers Of Babylon/Sunny/Ma Baker/Belfast/Rasputin/Brown Girl In The Ring/Hooray! Hooray! It's A Holi-Holiday/El Lute/Bahama Mama/I See A Boat On The River/Boonoonoonoos/Ribbons Of Blue/Gotta Go Home/Barbarella Fortuneteller/No Woman No Cry/Malaika/Todos Buenos/Rasputin (Fangoria)/*Ma Baker (The* Killer Barbies featuring Alaska)

Spain: Ariola 74321 38082 2 (1996).

16.09.96: peaked at no.**10**, charted for 13 weeks

Curiously, this Spanish compilation featured two recordings that weren't by Boney M. at all: a Spanish language electropop version of *Rasputin* by Fangoria, which samples Boney M.'s recording, plus a punk rock cover of *Ma Baker* by The Killer Barbies featuring Alaska.
    BEST IN SPAIN rose to no.10, and spent 13 weeks on the chart.

20 ~ *NORSKE HITS*

Daddy Cool/Ma Baker/Rivers Of Babylon/Brown Girl In The Ring/Hooray! Hooray! It's A Holi-Holiday/The Summer Mega Mix/Sunny/El Lute/Gotta Go Home/My Friend Jack/ Rasputin/Nightflight To Venus/Painter Man/Bahama Mama/Calendar Song/No Woman No Cry/Belfast/Fever/Kalimba De Luna

Norway: Hansa 74321 622622 (1997).

27.12.97: 32
14.11.98: 31-**17**-24-31-33-31-32-28-28-x-x-22-20-34

Another exclusive, this Boney M. compilation was only released in Norway, where on its initial release it spent a solitary week on the chart at no.32.

    Almost a year later, the album returned to the chart, and this time it rose to no.17 and spent 12 weeks on the chart.

21 ~ 20th CENTURY HITS

Sunny/Daddy Cool/Ma Baker/Rivers Of Babylon/Gotta Go Home/Rasputin/Painter Man/ No Woman No Cry/Brown Girl In The Ring/Hooray! Hooray! It's A Holi-Holiday/ Kalimba De Luna/Felicidad (Miami Ocean Drive Mix)/Mary's Boy Child / Oh My Lord/Caribbean Nightfever Megamix (Hooray! Hooray! It's A Holi-Holiday/Brown Girl In The Ring/No Woman No Cry/The Calendar Song)/Disco Megamix (Daddy Cool/Ma Baker/Sunny/Painter Man/Rivers Of Babylon/Belfast/Gotta Go Home/Rasputin)/Sunny (Club Mix)/Ma Baker (Club Mix)/Daddy Cool (Club Mix)/Rivers Of Babylon (Club Mix)/Gotta Go Home (Club Mix)

Germany: MCI 74321 70052 2 (1999).

22.11.99: **30**-41-35-50-70-84-65-87-93

UK: MCI 74321 70052 2 (1999).

20th CENTURY HITS wasn't a hit in the UK.

Finland
1.01.00: 22-**21**-27

France
15.01.00: 44-**38**-48-73-68

New Zealand
20.02.00: **50**

Spain
13.12.99: peaked at no.**17**, charted for 10 weeks

Sweden
28.10.99: 38-20
6.01.00: 38-11-**8**-9-17-26-37-38-50-51

Yet another remix album, *20th CENTURY HITS* was credited to Boney M. 2000.
    Remixes of *Ma Baker*, *Daddy Cool*, *Hooray! Hooray! It's A Holi-Holiday* and *Sunny* were all released as singles, some more successfully than others. The album itself sold reasonably well, and it achieved no.8 in Sweden, no.17 in Spain, no.21 in Finland, no.30 in Germany, no.38 in France and no.50 in New Zealand.

22 ~ 25 JAAR NA 'DADDY COOL' / GREATEST HITS

CD1: *Ma Baker/Sunny/Daddy Cool/Rivers Of Babylon/Rasputin/Painter Man/Belfast/No Woman No Cry/Brown Girl In The Ring/Hooray! Hooray! It's A Holi-Holiday/Gotta Go Home/Consuela Biaz/I See A Boat On The River/Felicidad (Margherita)/Baby Do You Wanna Bump/El Lute/I'm Born Again/Children Of Paradise/Mary's Boy Child / Oh My Lord*

CD2: *Rivers Of Babylon (Remix 2000 featuring Regi (Milk Inc.))/Gotta Go Home ('99 Remix)/Daddy Cool (Latino Club Mix)/Going Back West ('99 Remix)/Megamix (Radio Version) (Rivers Of Babylon/ Sunny/Daddy Cool/Ma Baker/Rasputin)/Brown Girl In The Ring ('93 Remix)/Happy Song/Kalimba De Luna/Papa Chico/We Kill The World (Don't Kill The World)/Bahama Mama/New York City/The Carnival Is Over (Goodbye True Lover)/Strange/My Friend Jack/Malaika/Ribbons Of Blue/Jambo – Hakuna Matata/Gadda Da Vida*

On later pressings *Rivers Of Babylon (Remix 2000 featuring Regi (Milk Inc.)* was replaced by *Ma Baker (Remix 1999 by Sash!).*

Belgium (Flanders): Paradiso PA 25876 (2001).

16.02.02: 20-**7**-10-15-33

Netherlands: BMG 74321 77782 2 (2000).

14.10.00: 57-**27**-32-40-57-50-58-71-68-74-82-92-92

This compilation, which was released in the Netherlands as *25 JAAR NA 'DADDY COOL' (25 Years After 'Daddy Cool')* and Belgium as *GREATEST HITS*, is notable because it featured the original album and 7" single versions of many of the featured songs.

Six songs on the compilation were making their CD debut, including two B-sides, *New York City* and *Strange*. The album also included a 1999 remix of *Going Back West* previously released exclusively in South Africa, plus a new remix of *Rivers Of Babylon* by Belgian band Milk Inc.'s Regi ~ the latter was issued as a single in the Netherlands, but it wasn't a hit.

25 JAAR NA 'DADDY COOL' charted at no.27 in the Netherlands, and more than a year later *GREATEST HITS* rose to no.7 in Belgium.

23 ~ THE COMPLETE COLLECTION

CD1: *Daddy Cool/Sunny/No Woman No Cry/Ma Baker/Love For Sale/Belfast/Have You Ever Seen The Rain/Still I'm Sad/Rivers Of Babylon/Brown Girl In The Ring/Heart Of Gold/Rasputin/Painter Man/Nightflight To Venus/Hooray! Hooray! It's A Holi-Holiday/El Lute/Gotta Go Home/I'm Born Again/Hold On I'm Coming/The Summer Mega Mix*

CD2: *The Calendar Song/Ribbons Of Blue/I See A Boat On The River/My Friend Jack/Children Of Paradise/Felicidad (Margherita)/Malaika/We Kill The World (Don't Kill The World)/I Shall Sing/The Carnival Is Over (Goodbye True Lover)/Jambo – Hakuna Matata/Happy Song/My Cherie Amor/Young, Free And Single/Dreadlock Holiday/Bang Bang Lulu/Feliz Navidad/Mary's Boy Child / Oh My Lord/White Christmas*

Denmark: BMG 74321 81195 2 (2000).

5.01.01: **21**-x-38-x-35-39

Like *25 JAAR NA 'DADDY COOL'* and *GREATEST HITS*, *THE COMPLETE COLLECTION* marked the 25th anniversary *Daddy Cool*. Released in Denmark only, where it charted at no.21. the 2CD compilation featured many original album and 7" versions. The track listing was more or less in chronological order, with the exception of three festive recordings that rounded off the album.

24 ~ THE MAGIC OF

Daddy Cool/Sunny/Rivers Of Babylon/El Lute/No Woman No Cry/Hooray! Hooray! It's A Holi-Holiday/Rasputin/Painter Man/Belfast/Brown Girl In The Ring/Kalimba De Luna/ Happy Song/Still I'm Sad/Mary's Boy Child / Oh My Lord/Baby, Do You Wanna Bump/ Felicidad (Margherita)/Gotta Go Home/Ma Baker/Sunny (2006 Remix)/A Moment Of Love

Germany: Sony BMG 88697 03262 2 (2006).

10.11.2006: 38-**19**-25-29-44-48-29-33-37-41-50-53-64-69-82-89-84-87-x-99

UK: Sony BMG 88697 034772 / 82876 89304 2 (2006).

9.12.06: 48-48-**45**-58

Australia
27.11.06: 68-**28**-33-38-37-46-66-85-57-81

Austria
 10.11.06: 19-**13**-18-23-32-40-25-21-32-36-25-25-42-46-64

Denmark
28.11.08: **16**-26-20-23-28-31-25

Finland
18.11.06: **27**-37

Netherlands
25.11.06: 98-x-x-97-**94**

New Zealand
6.11.06: 14-**5**-8-12-15-21-14-14-20-25-27-34-40

Norway
6.01.07: 7-3-**2-2-2**-4-5-7-7-17-24-25-27

Spain
4.03.07: 39-**23**-29-40-47-61-x-95-88-97
10.07.07: 97-70-63-71-71-83-99
30.03.08: 96-50-35-45-63-87-77-79-90
28.09.08: 48-64-96-86-82-78

Switzerland
12.11.06: 52-40-**39**-63-79-70-43-59-70-60-70-87-100

Not to be confused with the similarly titled 1980 compilation, this *THE MAGIC OF* album was essentially an up-dated version of 1992's *GOLD – 20 SUPER HITS*.

The album featured a new remix of *Sunny* by Mousse T., plus a brand new song *A Moment Of Love*, which was recorded in 2006 and featured Liz Mitchell. In the UK, the album was issued with an alternate track listing:

Rivers Of Babylon/Brown Girl In The Ring/Daddy Cool/Sunny/Mary's Boy Child / Oh My Lord/Rasputin/El Lute/Hooray! Hooray! It's A Holi-Holiday/No Woman No Cry/ Painter Man/Belfast/Kalimba De Luna/Happy Song/Still I'm Sad/Baby Do You Wanna Bump/Felicidad (Margherita)/Gotta Go Home/Ma Baker/Sunny (Mousse T. Remix)/A Moment Of Love

In Denmark, *THE MAGIC OF* was released as part of a 2CD package, with the 2007 festive compilation, *CHRISTMAS WITH*.

THE MAGIC OF charted at no.2 in Norway, no.5 in New Zealand, no.13 in Austria, no.16 in Denmark, no.19 in Germany, no.23 in Spain, no.27 in Finland, no.28 in Australia, no.39 in Switzerland and no.45 in the UK.

25 ~ CHRISTMAS WITH

Mary's Boy Child / Oh My Lord/When A Child Is Born/White Christmas/Feliz Navidad/ Jingle Bells/Zion's Daughter/Darkness Is Falling/Hark The Herald Angels Sing/Little Drummer Boy/The First Noel/Oh Christmas Tree/I'll Be Home For Christmas/Oh Come All Ye Faithful/Petit Papa Noel/Winter Fairy-Tale/Joy To The World/Auld Lang Syne/ Christmas Medley (Silent Night, Holy Night/Snow Falls Over The Ground/Hear Ye The Message/Sweet Bells)/Mary's Boy Child / Oh My Lord (Boney M. feat. Daddy Cool Kids)

Canada: *Christmas Medley & Mary's Boy Child / Oh My Lord* (Boney M. feat, Daddy Cool Kids) omitted.

Germany: MCI 88697 14032 2 (2007).

30.11.2007: 70-68-58-**57-57**

UK: Sony BMG 88697 14032 2 (2007).

CHRISTMAS WITH wasn't a hit in the UK.

Australia
23.12.07: 83-**46**-63

Austria
30.11.07: 58-42-**35**-37-37-47

Canada
28.11.15: 71-58-31-20-19-18-20
26.11.16: 90-56-39-29-18-**17**-34
2.12.17: 64-39-29-23-26-25-22
8.12.18: 75-40-41-37-30

New Zealand
10.12.07: 9-**6**-7-22

Spain
2.12.07: 89-87-**86**

Switzerland
9.12.07: **95**-98-99

Boney M.'s second festive compilation titled *CHRISTMAS WITH* brought together, for the first time, the 12 songs released on 1981's *CHRISTMAS ALBUM* and the six new songs recorded in 1984 for the cancelled *CHRISTMAS WITH* album (which was issued in South Africa only).

The album also featured a newly recorded version of *Mary's Boy Child / Oh My Lord*, featuring the Daddy Cool Kids.

CHRISTMAS WITH charted at no.6 in New Zealand, no.35 in Austria, no.46 in Australia and no.57 in Germany. In Canada, the album has entered the chart several times in recent years, peaking at no.18 on 2015, no.17 in 2016, no.22 in 2017 and no.30 in 2018.

26 ~ ULTIMATE 2.0

CD1 Classic Hits: *Daddy Cool/Rasputin/Rivers Of Babylon/Ma Baker/Hooray! Hooray! It's A Holi-Holiday/Sunny/Happy Song/Belfast/Brown Girl In The Ring/Kalimba De Luna/Felicidad/Mary's Boy Child / Oh My Lord/Baby Do You Wanna Bump/Painter Man/Gotta Go Home/No Woman No Cry/Sunny(Mousse T. Radio Mix)/A Moment Of Love*

CD2 Boney M. Goes Club: Barbra Streisand (Mega Mashup-Mix Medley vs. La Bouche, No Mercy, Chicken Soup*) (Barbra Streisand (The Most Wanted Woman)/Who The F**k Is Wikileaks/Daddy Cool/Sunny/Ma Baker/Happy Song/Sweet Dreams/Be My Lover/ Where Do You Go/Gotta Go Home)/Boney M. (Mega Mashup-Mix-Medley vs.* No Mercy, Eruption, La Bouche*) (Rivers Of Babylon/Missing/Where Do You Go/Kalimba De Luna/I See A Boat On The River/One Way Ticket/Sunny/Sweet Dreams)/Ma Baker (Club Mix)/Daddy Cool (Club Mix)/Sunny (Club Mix)/Rivers Of Babylon (Club Mix)/Gotta Go Home (Club Mix)/Rasputin (Club Mix)/Happy Song (Club Mix)/Barbra Streisand vs. Marilyn Monroe (Club Mix)/Who The F**k Is Wikileaks* (Chicken Soup vs. Boney M.)/*Be Bop A Lula (House Mix/Radio Edit)* (ZZ Queen vs. Boney M.)/*Barbra Streisand (Radio Edit* (Duck Sauce)

France: Sony 88697847942 (2011).

26.02.11: **28**-41-72

Belgium (Flanders)
5.03.11: 42-29-18-**14**-24-29-49-39-31-40-37-64-84-100

CD1 of this 2CD French release was titled 'Versions Originales', while CD2 was billed 'Boney M. Goes Club (Versions Remixees)'.

CD2 included a version of *Barbra Streisand (The Most Wanted Woman)*, plus the Radio Edit of Duck Sauce's hit version of the same song. Two mash-ups were featured, *Who The F**k Is Wikileaks*, credited to Chicken Soup Vs. Boney M., and Gene Vincent's *Be Bop A Lula*, credited to ZZ Queen Vs. Boney M.. Also featured were two songs by La Bouche (*Sweet Dreams* and *Be My Lover*), two songs by No Mercy (*Where Do You Go* and *Missing*) and Eruption's 1978 hit, *One Way Ticket*.

ULTIMATE 2.0 charted at no.28 in France, and at no.14 in the Flanders (French) region of Belgium.

27 ~ DIAMONDS

CD1: *Baby Do You Wanna Bump (Part I) (7" Version)/Daddy Cool/No Woman No Cry/Sunny/Ma Baker (7" Alternate Version)/Belfast/Rivers Of Babylon (7" Alternate Version)/Brown Girl In The Ring (7" Alternate Version)/Rasputin (7" Version)/Painter Man/Mary's Boy Child / Oh My Lord/Dancing In The Streets/Hooray! Hooray! It's A Holi-Holiday/Gotta Go Home (7" Version)/El Lute (7" Version)/Bahama Mama (7" Version)/I'm Born Again (Single Version)/I See A Boat On The River (7" Version)/My Friend Jack (7" Version)*

CD2: *Children Of Paradise/Gadda Da Vida (7" Version)/Felicidad (Margherita)/ Malaika/Consuela Biaz (7" Alternate Version)/We Kill The World (Don't Kill The World) (7" Version)/The Carnival Is Over (Goodbye True Lover) (7" Alternate Version)/Going Back West/Jambo – Hakuna Matata (No Problems)/Somewhere In The World (7" Version)/Exodus (Noah's Ark 2001) (7" Version)/Kalimba De Luna (7" Version)/Happy Song (7" Version)/My Cherie Amor/ Young, Free And Single/Bang Bang Lulu (7" Version)/Stories (Radio Mix)/Papa Chico (Rap Version)/Barbra Streisand (The Most Wanted Woman) (Radio Mix)*

CD3 New Hits & Mixes: *Song Of Joy (Single Edit)/Running Man (Frankie's On The Run)/Sunny (John Munich & Thorsten Skringer Radio Sax Edit)/Nightflight To Venus (Blank & Jones Remix)/Ma Baker (Blank & Jones Remix)/Daddy Cool (Nick Raider Radio Mix)/Kalimba De Luna (Bassflow De Luna Mix)/Rasputin (Bassflow 4.0 Mix)/Rivers Of Babylon (Echolot Mix)/Daddy Cool (Jay Frog & Amfree Remix)/Sunny (John Munich & Thorsten Skringer Extended Sax Mix)/Sunny (Blank & Jones Summer Vide Remix)/Rivers*

Of Babylon (Nick Raider Club Party Mix)/Kalimba De Luna (Instrumental – Bassflow De Luna Mix)/Rasputin (Instrumental – Bassflow Remix)

LP (Deluxe Edition only): *TAKE THE HEAT OFF ME* (original track listing).

DVD (Deluxe Edition only): Boney M. in Lammerspiel (94 minute concert)

Germany: 88875059992 / 88875076512 (Deluxe Edition) (2015).

13.04.15: 37-24-**20**-22-38-51-79

UK: not released.

Austria
10.04.15: 28-**19**-24-36-57-50

Switzerland
5.04.15: **30**-37-32-50

This 3CD box-set celebrated Boney M.'s 40th anniversary, with the first two CDs featuring a selection of the groups singles in chronological order ~ many in the 7" version or a 7" alternate version, plus a version of *Barbra Streisand*. The third CD was titled 'New Hits & Mixes', and featured a host of new remixes.

A deluxe edition of *DIAMONDS* was also released, which included the following extras:

- *TAKE THE HEAT OFF ME* vinyl album with original track listing
- DVD featuring a 94 minute concert at Lammerspiel, Germany.
- Black *Daddy Cool* T-shirt.

DIAMONDS charted at no.19 in Austria, no.20 in Germany and no.30 in Switzerland.

TOP 20 BONEY M. ALBUMS

This Top 20 Albums listing has been compiled according to the same points system used for the Top 40 Singles listing.

Rank/Album/Points

1 *NIGHTFLIGHT TO VENUS* – 2046 points

2 *LOVE FOR SALE* – 1797 points

3 *OCEANS OF FANTASY* – 1535 points

Rank/Album/Points

4   *TAKE THE HEAT OFF ME* – 1386 points

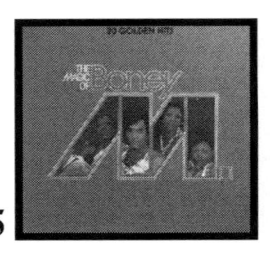

5   *THE MAGIC OF* (1980) – 1246 points

6. *THE MAGIC OF* (2006) – 785 points
7. *GOLD – 20 SUPER HITS* – 763 points
8. *BOONOONOONOOS* – 745 points
9. *20th CENTURY HITS* – 394 points
10. *CHRISTMAS WITH* (2007) – 320 points

11. *CHRISTMAS ALBUM* – 306 points
12. *DIAMONDS* – 207 points
13. *MORE GOLD 20 SUPER HITS VOL.II* – 205 points
14. *CHRISTMAS WITH* (1983) – 163 points
15. *TEN THOUSAND LIGHTYEARS* – 159 points
16. *25 JAAR NA 'DADDY COOL'* – 158 points
17. *32 SUPERHITS* – 150 points
18. *ULTIMATE 2.0* – 147 points
19. *THE VERY BEST OF* (1982) – 105 points
20. *BEST – SUPER SPECIAL ALBUM* – 91 points

Boney M.'s first four studio albums prove to be their most successful releases, with *NIGHTFLIGHT TO VENUS* taking first place from *LOVE FOR SALE*. The group's first international compilation, the first *THE MAGIC OF* release, rounds off the Top 5.

ALBUMS TRIVIA

To date, 27 Boney M. albums have achieved Top 40 status in one or more of the countries featured in this book, the majority of them compilations.

There follows a country-by-country look at the most successful Boney M. albums, starting with the group's homeland.

BONEY M. IN GERMANY

Boney M. achieved 15 hit albums in Germany, which charted for a total of 351 weeks.

No.1 Albums

1977	*LOVE FOR SALE*
1978	*NIGHTFLIGHT TO VENUS*
1979	*OCEANS OF FANTASY*

Most weeks at No.1

11 weeks	*NIGHTFLIGHT TO VENUS*
6 weeks	*LOVE FOR SALE*
2 weeks	*OCEANS OF FANTASY*

Albums with the most weeks

62 weeks	*LOVE FOR SALE*
61 weeks	*NIGHTFLIGHT TO VENUS*
56 weeks	*TAKE THE HEAT OFF ME*
37 weeks	*OCEANS OF FANTASY*
25 weeks	*THE MAGIC OF* (1980)
23 weeks	*GOLD – 20 SUPER HITS*
19 weeks	*THE MAGIC OF* (2006)
18 weeks	*BOONOONOONOOS*
14 weeks	*TEN THOUSAND LIGHTYEARS*

BONEY M. IN AUSTRALIA

Boney M. achieved 12 hit albums in Australia, which spent 177 weeks on the chart.

The group's most successful album in Australia is the 1980 compilation, *THE MAGIC OF*, which peaked at no.3.

Albums with the most weeks

41 weeks	*NIGHTFLIGHT TO VENUS*
40 weeks	*TAKE THE HEAT OFF ME*
22 weeks	*THE MAGIC OF* (1980)
16 weeks	*LOVE FOR SALE*
16 weeks	*OCEANS OF FANTASY*
13 weeks	*CHRISTMAS ALBUM*
10 weeks	*THE VERY BEST OF*
10 weeks	*THE MAGIC OF* (2006)

BONEY M. IN AUSTRIA

Boney M. achieved 10 hit albums in Austria, which spent 195 weeks on the chart.

No.1 Albums

1977	*LOVE FOR SALE*
1978	*NIGHTFLIGHT TO VENUS*
1979	*OCEANS OF FANTASY*

Most weeks at No.1

8 weeks	*LOVE FOR SALE*
8 weeks	*OCEANS OF FANTASY*
4 weeks	*NIGHTFLIGHT TO VENUS*

Albums with the most weeks

40 weeks	*LOVE FOR SALE*
36 weeks	*TAKE THE HEAT OFF ME*
36 weeks	*NIGHTFLIGHT TO VENUS*
20 weeks	*OCEANS OF FANTASY*
18 weeks	*THE MAGIC OF* (1980)
16 weeks	*GOLD – 20 SUPER HITS*
15 weeks	*THE MAGIC OF* (2006)

BONEY M. IN BELGIUM (Flanders)

Since 1995, when the Ultratop albums chart was launched, only two Boney M. albums have charted. The most successful was *GREATEST HITS*, which peaked at no.7.

BONEY M. IN CANADA

Between 1976 and 2000, and from 2015 onwards, Boney M. achieved six hit albums in Canada.

The group's most successful album during this period is *NIGHTFLIGHT TO VENUS*, which peaked at no.7.

Albums with the most weeks

31 weeks	*THE MAGIC OF* (1980)
26 weeks	*CHRISTMAS WITH*
17 weeks	*NIGHTFLIGHT TO VENUS*
11 weeks	*OCEANS OF FANTASY*
8 weeks	*CHRISTMAS ALBUM*

Note: Chart action from around 2000 to 2014 is missing, and pre-2000 chart action is incomplete.

BONEY M. IN DENMARK

Since 2001, two Boney M. album have charted in Denmark, with *THE MAGIC OF* (2006) proving the most successful, peaking at no.16.

Note: Chart action pre-2001 is missing.

BONEY M. IN FINLAND

Since 1995, two Boney M. album have charted in Finland, with *20th CENTURY HITS* proving the most successful, peaking at no.21.

Note: Chart action pre-1995 is missing.

BONEY M. IN FRANCE

Boney M. achieved seven hit albums in France, which spent 158 weeks on the chart.

No.1 Albums

1977	*LOVE FOR SALE*
1979	*OCEANS OF FANTASY*

Both albums spent just one week at no.1.

Albums with the most weeks

48 weeks	*NIGHTFLIGHT TO VENUS*
40 weeks	*LOVE FOR SALE*
34 weeks	*TAKE THE HEAT OFF ME*
24 weeks	*OCEANS OF FANTASY*
5 weeks	*20th CENTURY HITS*

BONEY M. IN JAPAN

Boney M. achieved four hit albums in Japan, which spent 61 weeks on the chart.

The group's most successful album is the compilation *BEST – SUPER SPECIAL ALBUM*, which peaked at no.15.

Albums with the most weeks

21 weeks	*BEST – SUPER SPECIAL ALBUM*
15 weeks	*TAKE THE HEAT OFF ME*
14 weeks	*NIGHTFLIGHT TO VENUS*
11 weeks	*OCEANS OF FANTASY*

BONEY M. IN THE NETHERLANDS

Boney M. achieved ten hit albums in the Netherlands, which spent 163 weeks on the chart.

No.1 Albums

1978	*NIGHTFLIGHT TO VENUS*

NIGHTFLIGHT TO VENUS spent five weeks at no.1.

Albums with the most weeks

35 weeks	*GOLD – 20 SUPER HITS*
30 weeks	*NIGHTFLIGHT TO VENUS*
24 weeks	*OCEANS OF FANTASY*
21 weeks	*THE MAGIC OF* (1980)
16 weeks	*LOVE FOR SALE*
13 weeks	*25 JAAR NA 'DADDY COOL'*
11 weeks	*TAKE THE HEAT OFF ME*

BONEY M. IN NEW ZEALAND

Boney M. achieved ten hit albums in New Zealand, which spent 145 weeks on the chart.

The group's most successful album is *GOLD – 20 SUPER HITS*, which spent five weeks at no.2. *THE MAGIC OF* (1980) also peaked at no.2, but only for a solitary week.

Albums with the most weeks

47 weeks	*NIGHTFLIGHT TO VENUS*
35 weeks	*GOLD – 20 SUPER HITS*
17 weeks	*THE MAGIC OF* (1980)
14 weeks	*OCEANS OF FANTASY*
13 weeks	*THE MAGIC OF* (2006)

BONEY M. IN NORWAY

Boney M. achieved nine hit albums in Norway, which spent 179 weeks on the chart.

No.1 Albums

1978	*NIGHTFLIGHT TO VENUS*
1979	*OCEANS OF FANTASY*

Both albums topped the chart for two weeks.

Albums with the most weeks

45 weeks	*TAKE THE HEAT OFF ME*
30 weeks	*LOVE FOR SALE*
30 weeks	*NIGHTFLIGHT TO VENUS*
19 weeks	*OCEANS OF FANTASY*

14 weeks	*BOONOONOONOOS*
13 weeks	*NORSKE HITS*
13 weeks	*THE MAGIC OF* (2006)
10 weeks	*GOLD – 20 SUPER HITS*

BONEY M. IN SOUTH AFRICA

Post-1981, Boney M. achieved four hit albums in South Africa, which spent 58 weeks on the chart.

The group's most successful album is *BOONOONOONOOS*, which peaked at no.2.

Albums with the most weeks

25 weeks	*THE VERY BEST OF*
24 weeks	*BOONOONOONOOS*
8 weeks	*CHRISTMAS WITH*

Note: the official South African album chart didn't commence until December 1981.

BONEY M. IN SPAIN

Boney M. achieved ten hit albums in Spain, which spent 208 weeks on the chart.

No.1 Albums

1977	*TAKE THE HEAT OFF ME*
1977	*LOVE FOR SALE*
1978	*NIGHTFLIGHT TO VENUS*
1979	*OCEANS OF FANTASY*

Most Weeks at No.1

7 weeks	*LOVE FOR SALE*
4 weeks	*OCEANS OF FANTASY*

Albums with the most weeks

42 weeks	*LOVE FOR SALE*
34 weeks	*NIGHTFLIGHT TO VENUS*
31 weeks	*THE MAGIC OF* (2006)
28 weeks	*TAKE THE HEAT OFF ME*

25 weeks	*OCEANS OF FANTASY*
21 weeks	*BOONOONOONOOS*
13 weeks	*BEST IN SPAIN*
10 weeks	*20th CENTURY HITS*

BONEY M. IN SWEDEN

Boney M. achieved eight hit albums in Sweden, which spent 149 weeks on the chart.

No.1 Albums

1976	*TAKE THE HEAT OFF ME*
1977	*LOVE FOR SALE*
1978	*NIGHTFLIGHT TO VENUS*

Most weeks at No.1

10 weeks	*LOVE FOR SALE*
8 weeks	*NIGHTFLIGHT TO VENUS*
6 weeks	*TAKE THE HEAT OFF ME*

Albums with the most weeks

46 weeks	*TAKE THE HEAT OFF ME*
28 weeks	*LOVE FOR SALE*
26 weeks	*OCEANS OF FANTASY*
24 weeks	*NIGHTFLIGHT TO VENUS*
12 weeks	*20th CENTURY HITS*

BONEY M. IN SWITZERLAND

Boney M. achieved ten hit albums in Switzerland, which spent 168 weeks on the chart.

No.1 Albums

1977	*LOVE FOR SALE*
1978	*NIGHTFLIGHT TO VENUS*
1979	*OCEANS OF FANTASY*

Most Weeks at No.1

6 weeks	*LOVE FOR SALE*
4 weeks	*NIGHTFLIGHT TO VENUS*
2 weeks	*OCEANS OF FANTASY*

Albums with the most weeks

50 weeks	*LOVE FOR SALE*
24 weeks	*NIGHTFLIGHT TO VENUS*
22 weeks	*TAKE THE HEAT OFF ME*
18 weeks	*THE MAGIC OF* (1980)
14 weeks	*GOLD – 20 SUPER HITS*
13 weeks	*THE MAGIC OF* (2006)
10 weeks	*OCEANS OF FANTASY*
10 weeks	*BOONOONOONOOS*

BONEY M. IN THE UNITED KINGDOM

Boney M. achieved nine hit albums in the UK, which spent 147 weeks on the chart.

No.1 Albums

1978	*NIGHTFLIGHT TO VENUS*
1979	*OCEANS OF FANTASY*
1980	*THE MAGIC OF*

Most weeks at No.1

4 weeks	*NIGHTFLIGHT TO VENUS*
2 weeks	*THE MAGIC OF* (1980)
1 week	*OCEANS OF FANTASY*

Albums with the most weeks

65 weeks	*NIGHTFLIGHT TO VENUS*
26 weeks	*THE MAGIC OF* (1980)
18 weeks	*GOLD – 20 SUPER HITS*
10 weeks	*LOVE FOR SALE*
10 weeks	*THE GREATEST HITS*

BRIT/BPI (British Phonographic Industry) Awards

The BPI began certifying albums in 1973, and between April 1973 and December 1978, awards related to a monetary value and not a unit value. Thanks to inflation, this changed several times over the years:

- April 1973 – August 1974: Silver = £75,000, Gold = £150,000, Platinum = £1 million.
- September 1974 – December 1975: Gold raised to £250,000, others unchanged.
- January 1976 – December 1976: Silver raised to £100,000, others unchanged.
- January 1977 – December 1978: Silver raised to £150,000, Gold raised to £300,000, Platinum unchanged.

When this system was abolished, the awards that were set remain in place today: Silver = 60,000, Gold = 100,000, Platinum = 300,000. Multi-Platinum awards were introduced in February 1987. *Note:* the certification levels were double for budget albums before July 2013.

In July 2013 the BPI automated awards, and awards from this date are based on actual sales since February 1994, not shipments.

Platinum	*NIGHTFLIGHT TO VENUS* (September 1978)	= £1 million
Platinum	*OCEANS OF FANTASY* (February 1980)	= 300,000
Gold	*LOVE FOR SALE* (July 1978)	= £300,000
Gold	*THE MAGIC OF* (1980) (May 1980)	= 100,000
Gold	*THE MAGIC OF* (2006) (July 2013)	= 100,000
Gold	*THE BEST OF* (July 2013)	= 100,000
Silver	*TAKE THE HEAT OFF ME* (July 1978)	= £150,000
Silver	*THE GREATEST HITS* (July 2013)	= 60,000

BONEY M. IN THE UNITED STATES OF AMERICA

Only one Boney M. album has entered the Billboard 200 in the USA, *NIGHTFLIGHT TO VENUS* ~ it peaked at no.134 and charted for 10 weeks.

BONEY M. IN ZIMBABWE

Boney M. achieved eight hit albums in Zimbabwe.

No.1 Albums

1978   *RIVERS OF BABYLON* (aka *NIGHTFLIGHT TO VENUS*)
1980   *THE MAGIC OF*

Most Weeks at No.1

11 weeks   *THE MAGIC OF*
 2 weeks   *RIVERS OF BABYLON*

Note: the number of weeks each album spent on the chart in Zimbabwe isn't known.

Printed in Great Britain
by Amazon